Less Blah-Blah More Ah-Ha

How social savvy real estate agents become trusted, preferred, referred – and rewarded.

By Ken Brand

To my brothers and sisters in the real estate business, I wish you grace, speed, and sweet success.

Keep the faith.

ACKNOWLEDGMENTS

It's a minor miracle that you're reading this book. No way I ever could have accomplished this without the monstrous individual gestures of support, encouragement, and an occasional kick in the butt from my friends and family.

First, thank you to my wife of twenty-eight years, Robyn and our kids, Lauren, Nick and Heather. Without your encouragement to keep the faith and keep writing, I never would have finished. You guys have always been my biggest supporters; you were my tiger-blood difference makers.

Workwise, there are so many I've learned from. I don't have enough room to list everyone, and I hope you'll forgive me if your name does not appear here. The following people have had a profound impact on my career, and thus on the book. Mom and Dad — who knew, right? Thank you Joe Vane,

Sandy Bassler, Charles Marsh, Mac Bintliff, Marilyn Eiland, Mark Woodroof, Linda Sawyers, Greg and Michele Flory and Roger and Lupe Davila.

Writerwise, it's completely ironic that I've written a book. As a kid I loved to read, but hated and avoided all writing projects in school. My desire to write was kindled and shaped by my friends and teachers at The Wizard Academy in Austin, Texas. Thank you Roy H. Williams, Jeff Sexton, Chris Maddux, and fellow tribe members — without your example and encouragement, we wouldn't be reading this.

Thanks Dr. Liz Alexander for being my Book Doula and transforming my supremely raw and uncut diamond into something I'm proud of.

I'd like to express my heartfelt thanks to Benn and Lani Rosales for allowing me to share and shape many of the ideas you'll find in this book on their award-winning online magazine at AgentGenius.com. Their support and the constructive comments of my fellow AG readers were key in helping me to crystallize and express my thoughts and ideas. Thanks, man.

Lastly, thanks to my REALTOR Icon Tribe members at Prudential Gary Greene REALTORS®, and our Research Forest Office in The Woodlands, Texas. Where would I be without you beautiful souls? Nowhere. Thanks[10]. Cheers.

FOREWORD

It was 1994 when we acquired an office in The Woodlands. As I set out to find the perfect leader, Ken Brand's name came up again and again. I suspect that this book and all the Ah Ha moments the reader will experience will spread his fame even further.

Let's face it. Perpetual superstardom in real estate is elusive at best. So when you see a leader that can orchestrate the evolution of his team into consistent high performers, you know he is on to something. Ken Brand has not only figured it out, he has a most engaging and irreverent way to explain what to do, how to do it, and why.

When email was just beginning to take its place, front and center, in our lives, Ken's special talent for nudging his team in the right direction became evident. The night before his weekly sales meeting he sent an email inviting them to breakfast on him at a local spot. The breakfast was to replace the meeting. You can probably guess the outcome but that was the day the journey began, from attachments to YouTube to Facebook and Twitter and SlideShare and all that social media has to offer.

I have never known anyone in real estate who loves to learn more than Ken and that he wants to share what he has learned is our good fortune. Keeping the 'new world' consumer in the forefront, he shows us how to use the technology to gain and maintain top of mind awareness. If you want to be a real estate professional perpetually connected, trusted, chosen and referred, read this book!

Marilyn Eiland, President
Prudential Gary Greene, Realtors
February 2011

TABLE OF CONTENTS

INTRODUCTION

It was 1978. I was twenty-two, a brand new real estate agent and out-loud clueless. Supremely green, I showed up at the office almost every day around 10 a.m. I arrived embarrassingly enthusiastic, I ~~hoped and prayed~~ believed today was the day something lucky and magically amazing would happen to me because I was a good person. Which of course it never did — because hope, no matter how enthusiastic, and praying for good luck, are doomed success strategies.

Natalie, our sales manager, knew this, of course; she ~~took pity on me~~ took me under her motherly wing and set me in motion: "Get to work, Kenny. Get out of the office, go knock on doors; go somewhere, anywhere – start handing out your business cards. By the boxful!" So I did.

My first sale came just six days later. I'd been handing out my freshly-printed Mr. Big Shot business cards when Muriel, the general manager at my gym, asked if I knew the La Costa area. She and her boyfriend wanted to buy a home there. I'd never been to La Costa, but I knew where it was: thirty-seven miles up the Pacific Coast Highway. I said, "Sure, I know LaCosta like the back of my hand – let's go look this weekend." Muriel said, "Okay."

I went to work. Thumbing through our fat San Diego MLS book, I found what I was looking for in the very back of the book. In a tiny two-page section titled *Out of the Area*, I found three properties that matched Muriel's criteria.

Not wanting to get lost or look lame with clients in tow, I set up Friday afternoon property preview appointments to learn the route and inspect the properties. While touring I noticed *For Sale* signs in every neighborhood. I thought that was weird; only two tiny pages in the book, yet so many *For Sale* signs? Huh? Hmmm? Whatever. Hustling forward, windows rolled down, eight-track blaring, I finished my tour and headed home.

Saturday morning came and went. Muriel and her boyfriend fell in love with the first home we saw. The seller accepted our full price offer and I had my first sale. Boom goes the dynamite!

I swaggered in early for our next sales meeting. Early enough to brag around the office about my awesomeness and how easy I thought selling real estate was. I must have mentioned how there were only three properties to show because instead of hip-hip-hooray and high fives, there were side-long glances, nervous laughter, and a smattering of disapproving headshakes.

Turns out, the reason that there were only three suitable properties listed in the MLS book was because La Costa wasn't in San Diego County. La Costa fell into an entirely different Multiple Listing Service Area, which had its own REALTOR Association and thousands-of-properties-thick MLS book. I had thought *Out of the Area* meant that it was a long drive away. DOH!

Luckily my clients LOVED their new place and my utter inexperience didn't harm them. But I knew I needed to wise up. So I did.

Except...

The sale closed in thirty-two days and my first commission check was a princely $2,700. Woo-hoo! Before passing the real estate exam I had earned $106 a week as a drive-through teller at the Hillcrest Branch of Bank of America. What do you think a 22-year-old knucklehead was going to do with the sudden lump sum equivalent of twenty-five weeks of bank teller pay? You're right. ~~Parrrttyyyyy~~ Everything but *work*.

After squandering my money, I returned to the office eager to collect my next big commission check. I was still hoping harder than I worked and quickly came to realize that my lonesome sale was the result of dumb luck, that the business wasn't easy, and I definitely wasn't awesome. I was right back where I started: ignorant, frustrated — and out of money.

I knew I had to get my act together or it was back to banker's hours for me, cashing other people's checks and taking — instead of making—bank deposits. So I did.

Serendipity and Elephant Ears

Fast-forward a few months.

In those days, private offices for top producers didn't exist. Serendipity planted me in a cubicle next to Sandy Felspar, a living real estate legend. She sold dozens of houses a year, carried an inventory of over twenty listings at all times, out-worked, out-charmed, and out-produced every agent in the Clairemont/Mission Bay marketplace. I was still supremely inexperienced, but I wasn't stupid. So I acted casual and paid strict attention to Sandy. Things were about to change.

Whenever Sandy worked her phone following up with clients, calling expired listings, answering sign calls, cold calling, and negotiating contracts — I stopped what I was doing, put on my elephant ears, and listened *real hard*. That wasn't all. I watched what she did and how she did it.

Sandy wasn't the only real estate agent I eavesdropped on. We had fifty-seven cubicles and our office was full. I listened with intent, kept an open mind, and took notes. Along with Sandy's rockstar lessons, I learned what not to do from the loose cannons, the mediocre, and the plain lazy.

Mind Sets, Skill Sets and Mediocre Selling Styles

What I learned from Sandy was that she listened more than she talked, and asked way more questions than the other real estate agents I watched. Whenever phone conversations turned tense, the other agents would react defensively — aggressively, arrogantly, or just plain ignorantly. Sandy didn't react, she responded. Calmly. Her conversations remained firmly confident and silky smooth. Sandy's focus was always on other people; she cared more about her relationships with them than how great and famous everyone thought she was. Her sensitive approach and focus on people, rather than deals and units, along with hard smart work, created a neverending conga line of new, repeat, and referred customers and clients.

In the Years That Followed

Thanks to Sandy and all the other real estate agents who influenced me — both superstars and secret agents—I've notched up some pretty impressive accolades of my own. Since those early days, I've been involved in over 17,000 real estate transactions. I've led, managed, trained, and mentored hundreds of new and experienced real estate agents in San Diego, Austin, Aspen, and The Woodlands, Texas. I've survived three real estate depressions and as many booms. I've seen mortgage rates spike as high as 22% and free fall as low as 3.5%. I've collaborated, commiserated, and competed with renowned top producers and thought-leaders in the business. I've received awards as an individual, as well as a member of and the leader of winning teams.

Most importantly, what I've learned is that the real estate business isn't about self, sticks, bricks, and stucco houses. I've learned that the key to modern success in our industry depends on earning trust, consistent high performance, and the willingness to adapt to current cultural and societal values, expectations, fears, and desires.

Today we live in a don't-bore-me, don't-bullshit-me, and definitely-don't-sell-me society. The old ways of bragging, chasing, capturing, closing, and strong-arm selling don't work. Today we create success through sharing, solving, supporting, and serving others. To help real estate agents navigate their way to new success in our new world, I've written this very different kind of ~~sales~~ guidebook.

All told, the best of my thirty-two years of experience is shared here. You'll find lessons and straightforward action steps and strategies that will create renewed relationships, Top of Mind Awareness, trust, opportunity, self-respect, and sweet success.

This Book Is for YOU If You Relate to One or All These Three Groups

Group One

Lifelong Learners are always stretching, growing, and searching for interesting ways to renew and enhance their value. What you guys love and value most of all is what psychologists call "intrinsically motivated" stuff: it's all about the good feelings you get from a job well done. The strategies in this book are my way of contributing to your ongoing curiosity and desire to excel for its own sake. By taking the advice in this book to heart and putting it into action, you'll benefit mentally, creatively, and professionally.

Group Two

Aspirationals also like to soak up new information, engage in new experiences, and move forward toward mastery. It's just that you are motivated a little differently. Psychologists describe you as being "extrinsically motivated"—by money, acclaim, winning all those awards, and feelings of pride and accomplishment. Hey, nothing wrong with that; it's all good, but you can win even bigger! This is why I'm offering you some new ways of thinking and acting that will help you glide to higher, more tangibly rewarding levels of success.

Group Three

Temporary Strugglers: Feel frustrated and stuck? You're determined to succeed, but no matter how hard you work, affirm, and strive, it seems your sincere efforts lead to dead-end rejection, fatigue, stress, and stuck-going-nowhere depression. What I want to assure you is this: It's not your fault!! More importantly, there's nothing wrong with *you*. The problem is, you've been taught, or you've on-your-own stumbled into the soul-sucking quicksand of doing the wrong things with the wrong people at the wrong time.

What worked in the 1990s — or even three years ago — doesn't work in today's real estate world. Chasing strangers, annoying your friends, and practicing insensitive and selfish selling styles are shunned by everyone, everywhere. Sadly, this style of selling is as common as bad news, and real estate careers across the country are doomed because of it. Extra sadly, most training programs are way behind the times. Consumer demands, preferences, and expectations have moved forward but traditional sales training and taught activities and actions haven't kept pace.

Thankfully, creating personal success doesn't require a diploma in rocket-surgery. In fact, to soar, you already have everything you need—right here, right now. You have the mental makeup and the strength to succeed. Plus, you have this book crammed with bright ideas and modern concepts that have helped thousands of real estate agents — no smarter or better-looking or funnier or more charming than you — to succeed. These folks are already enjoying the personal rewards of respect, trust, sweet success, and six-figure incomes. Let me show you how you can, too.

How to Use This Book

Perpetual success isn't an accident; it occurs only on purpose. This book was created to help you create the success you want to see in three distinct and easily implementable Success Stages. The content of this book has been organized around each of them.

In Stage One, you will discover the philosophical foundations for becoming more visible, choosable, and generating more referrals. In Chapters One to Eight you will learn precisely what business you are *really* in; The Two True Secrets to Success; and the high-impact dynamics of **Top of Mind Awareness**.

However, it's not enough just to know *what* to do. Most of the time we fail to succeed because we keep getting in our own way. Stage Two acknowledges and addresses the self-imposed emotional and mental obstacles that stop us moving forward. In Chapters Nine through Thirteen, you will discover how to face and conquer your fears and slay self-doubt; why it's wise to use psychographics to connect with your tribes, networks, and niches; and what The Golden Rule 2.0 is all about, and why we can't win without it.

Once we know how and why things work and how to get out of our own way, it's time to apply some practical, simple-to-follow ideas that will help you attract, discover, and create new opportunities. Stage Three (Chapters Fourteen to Twenty-Four) provides you with forty instantly implementable action events that put everything you've learned into play.

Within a number of the chapters you will find exercises that will not only help embed the material but provide you with personalized insights on moving forward to become omnipresent, attractive, choosable, and referrable. It's tempting to skip these exercises, I know. But if you want to get the most out of this book, I urge you to carve out and invest that small amount of time really identifying what more you can do to achieve the outcomes you want in your business.

Einstein is credited with coining the definition of insanity as "Doing the same thing over and over again, expecting a different result." In today's hyper-competitive real estate business, competition and consumer expectations are ripping and roiling with change. If Einstein were alive today, I believe he'd approve of this second definition for the real estate business. Here's my version:, "The definition of insanity is doing the same thing over and over again and expecting the same result." You see, if our prospects, suspects, clients, and competitors are continuously upping the ante, and we stand pat, doing the same old things in the same old Blah-Blah boring ways we're utterly screwed. Thankfully, your amazing talents, plus what you learn and implement from this book, will earn you perpetual success, pride, and profitability. Your clients will love you, and you'll have fun, too.

But Before We Get Started...

Let me ask you a question. It's a question that is asked in various ways. It's asked in agent interviews, business planning sessions, and workshops. New and experienced agents ask it too. Even curious civilians ask. Want to know what it is? Just turn the page.

STAGE I:

Fundamental Laws of Human Behavior

"I've learned that people will forget what you said, people will forget what you did, but people will never forget how you made them feel."

– Maya Angelou

Chapter One

What it takes to succeed in real estate?

My answer is what I call **The True Two Secrets to Success.** They are:

Knowing What Others Don't

and

Doing What Others Won't

That's it. It's that simple. Or rather, it's simple to understand. To create success takes diligent effort. To succeed, both knowing what others don't and doing what the average and ordinary won't are absolute requirements. To help internalize these two secrets, let's look at them individually.

Knowing What Others Don't

The more you know, the more attractive and valuable you are to other people (buyers and sellers). Ask yourself: "What do I know that others don't? What do the achievers I admire know that I don't: about marketing, social media, building trust, problem solving, market knowledge, technical knowledge, communication, listening and presentation?"

You and I both know that the permanently successful are always learning, reinventing themselves, and continuously upgrading what they do and how they do it. It bums me out that legions of hopeful achievers don't understand the definition of insanity: "If you always do what you've always done, you'll always get what you've always gotten." One simple key to victory and satisfaction is knowing that if you want a bigger and better result, you have to change, enhance, upgrade, or otherwise reinvent yourself. Then you have to take the new you and propel yourself into boom-goes-the-dynamite action.

Seriously, it's illogical and frankly impossible to go from status quo to sweet new success by doing the same tired old things over and over and over again. If we want to create continual, sustained success, we have to know more about *what works now* than our competitors. With this book, you're off and running. Keep going. . . learn, learn, learn.

Doing What Others Won't

It's pretty straightforward. Without action, our good intentions are nothing more than cool-sounding ideas. To turn bright ideas and good intentions into new and tangible success, we gotta stop making *getting-ready-to-get-ready* excuses, lift our butts off the couch and focus on DOING smart things. Bottom line: to succeed you have got to take dramatic, boom-goes-the-dynamite action in this area as well. Especially when it scares you.

What Holds You Back

Ok, about now you might be thinking, it's easy to talk about doing things others won't do, but it's very, very hard to actually do what scares you. I get that, because even after thirty-two years in the business, I'm just like everyone else. I still experience icy waves of fear and self-doubt. And on occasion, I struggle to avoid getting sucked and suckered into feel-good, but unproductive and unprofitable, creative avoidance activities. What I've learned is that fear feelings are normal in the real estate business. The difference between the perpetually successful and the perpetually struggling is their ability to take action even when their hearts and imaginations are pounding with fear. I've learned that while doing unfamiliar things may cause us to stumble and temporarily fail, ultimately we learn and grow. In this book you'll learn how to overcome self-imposed barriers and position yourself to be the *most* choosable agent among your peers.

Now, before we move to Chapter Two, let me ask you a question. What business do you think we are in? What's that? The real estate business, you say?

WRONG! We are absolutely NOT in the real estate business.

For the true answer, read on.

Chapter Two

Surprise! We're Not in the Real Estate Business

"Any opportunity to be helpful is an opportunity to earn money."

– Chris Brogan, Trust Agents

I love eating out. In particular, I love to eat dinner at Fleming's Steak House. If you haven't been, you should go. Now, in Houston, Texas where I live there's a steak house on every other corner. They all cook steak and serve cocktails. So I have plenty of choices, right? But I choose Fleming's first. Why?

Well, before I answer that question, let's consider the *real* business of a steak house. Is it to cook steak and sling drinks? Nope.

If they crave raving and returning fans, Yelps, word of mouth recommendations, and profits, the *real* business of a supreme steak house like Fleming's is to serve up *remarkable experiences*, to soothe us with the *visual delights* of their decor, to *tongue tease* with dishes that are unique to them (you must order the Chocolate Lava Cake), and to make sure every customer leaves the place impressed and *feeling good*. Even though the word "steak" is included in the name of their establishment, at Fleming's it's not all about the steak. It's about the entire *feel good experience*, which just happens to include a sizzling steak. When I and countless others dine at Fleming's Steakhouse, we're not just being sold steak and vodka gimlets, we're *buying* a memorable and pleasurable experience.

Fleming's, like Apple, Starbucks, Louboutin, and all those other iconic brands we love, know what business they're in. And believe me, it's not simply about steak, digital devices, coffee, and shoes. It's about the customer experience; in particular, how experiencing these brands make us *feel*. Feelings that include desire, lust, and appreciation.

So let me ask again:

What Business Are You and I in?

Most real estate agents would say that we're in the business of listing, selling, and closing real estate transactions. Right?

Nope. Nada. WRONG!!!

Selling a house is the end result of a transaction, but client delight and our long-term success happen only when we focus on the *total client experience.* The total client experience, Blah Blah or Ooh La La, is shaped by the quality of our communication, presentation, sharing, problem solving, and service. I guess you could say the *total client experience* we deliver is a reflection of our values: what we believe in, what we stand for, and where we choose to draw the line between common and uncommon.

Here's the deal. To set a firm foundation for your future, we need to determine if your current efforts are focused on selling houses and doing deals, or delivering client-centered service and wow-whee experiences? So let's begin by asking ourselves the following questions to reveal where our heads are.

The following are Blah-Blah Boring and Ah-Ha and Appreciated comparison charts. Either put a physical mark or a mental check against each of these statements, then total them up to discover whether your thinking lies mainly in the "Blah Blah" or the "Ah Ha and Appreciated":

How are we communicating?

Blah Blah Boring	Ah-Ha and Appreciated
It's all about YOU and how great you are.	It's all about how you can support and serve others.
You talk-talk-talk, mostly about yourself and how great you are.	You ask questions and listen-listen-listen for clues on how best to serve them.
Personality-free monologue broadcasts, i.e., direct mail, e-mail and print advertising.	Two-way conversation and engagement, i.e., in person, Facebook, chat, text, etc.
Your way, at your convenience.	Tailor-made as they desire, expect and deserve.
BS sales speak, acronyms, and subtle condescension.	Simple, accurate, and respectful.

How are we presenting ourselves and what impressions and perceptions are we creating?

Blah Blah Boring	Ah-Ha and Appreciated
Amateur, cheap, and Jurassic.	Professional, attractive, and modern.
Unsure, whiny, nervous, and pessimistic.	Confident, assured, patient, and optimistic.
Uninformed, unprepared, and ignorant.	Knowledgeable, prepared, and savvy.
Bragging and telling them.	Sharing and showing them.
Focused on YOU.	Focused on THEM.

How do we solve problems?

Blah Blah Boring	Ah-Ha and Appreciated
Rigid and self-centered.	Flexible and client-centric.
Defensive, aggressive, and uncertain.	Receptive, calm, and confident.
Passive and procrastination- prone.	Engaged, enthusiastic and action-oriented.
Condescending and flippant.	Respectful and courteous.

How do we share and support others?

Blah Blah Boring	Ah-Ha and Appreciated
Taking more than you give.	Giving more than you take.
Stingy	Generous
Hoarding your knowledge and information.	Sharing your knowledge and information online, i.e., Facebook.com, blogging, SlideShare.net, Youtube.com,

How do we lead and inspire others?

Blah Blah Boring	Ah-Ha and Appreciated
Negative and impatient attitude.	Positive and patient attitude.
Over promise and under deliver.	Keep your commitments and over deliver.
Fly by the seat of your pants.	Follow a proven system.
Avoid problems, blame others, and make excuses.	Respond proactively, fix mistakes, respect others, and accept responsibility.
Wait and hesitate.	Take swift and confident action.

Okay, I'm a realistic guy. I know you probably skimmed through that chart without seriously inspecting your *total client experience* foundation. I'll assume that's because you're so stoked about finding new what-to-do's in this book that you thought this could be skipped over. But, please: this will take you only three minutes, five tops. Go back and review each question, think about it critically, and answer honestly. You don't have to share your results; most definitely don't criticize yourself. What this exercise will help you do is to see which old habits are holding you back and what needs changing.

Once you've decided on what you're committed to improving, then and only then can you begin to consciously include new, positive traits concerning aspects of your communication, presentation, sharing, solutions, and leadership styles.

So, bearing in mind that people mostly make new decisions based on new information, let me ask you again:

What business are you really in?

Jot down your answer as a personal mini Values Statement on an index card or a yellow sticky note and keep it in your purse or wallet. Review it daily. That way you will be reminded that the real estate business is about things that are way more meaningful than simply selling houses.

But, you might be asking, why do I need to think this way? What are the benefits of changing what countless real estate professionals have been trained to think, do and feel for decades? Let's look at the reasons *why* we need to re-think the business we are in. It's a five-letter word. Can you guess what it is? Read on...

Chapter Three

Earning True-Blue Trust and Credibility

"One can never be sure what a deserted area looks like."

~ George Carlin

Still thinking about that five-letter word? See if this state-of-current-business-affairs overview offers any clues.

Civilians are polite people, they don't say it out loud, but they think it: *Real estate agents are full of excrement.*

Harris Poll Interactive conducted a nationwide telephone survey in 2009 and asked the following question about a number of different occupations:

"For each (of these occupations), would you tell me if you feel it is an occupation of very great prestige, considerable prestige, some prestige, or hardly any prestige at all?"

Of the twenty-three occupations that were included in Harris's list, Real Estate Agent/Broker came in dead last in terms of prestige. In case you're curious, firefighter topped the list and lawyer (who'd have thought it?) placed roughly in the middle at #13.

Now why do real estate agents fare so poorly?

Well, let's be honest here. It's hardly any wonder that civilians view real estate agents as a necessary evil. For decades most of us have behaved out-loud self-centered. We boast about how awesome we are, screaming I'm Number One! Dig ME!! Dig MY awards!!! Dig MY billboards!!!! Traditionally, real estate agents waste more money on personally promoting *themselves* than they spend on promoting the properties of their clients.

Many real estate agents charge a lot and do little. For example, are you familiar with this scenario?

1. List the property.

2. Plant a rusty-framed *For Sale* sign in the front yard.

3. Throw the property into the MLS system: Upload lame pictures and an even worse property description.

4. Lie low, do as little as possible, and pray that it sells.

5. Collect a fat commission check for doing next to nothing.

Let's face it friends, even when success is achieved, clients are often left with feelings of frustration and bamboozlement as to why it cost them so much for so little effort. So who can blame civilians for viewing real estate agents in a dim and untrustworthy light? Not me.

So we have two huge challenges here. The first is to overcome decades of negative perspectives about our profession. The second is to swim against the tide of traditional self-centered and irresponsible real estate agent behavior.

To meet the challenge and ensure our immediate and consistent success, we must be perceived as trustworthy and credible. Without trust, we're doomed. With trust we become *choosable* and — even more important to our long-term success — we become referrable. The only way to be perceived as trustworthy is to actually behave in trustworthy ways.

Oh, and yeah, *trust* is that five-letter word I wanted you to come up with.

Trust

Now I know that you know that *trust* is important in business. Where I see many real estate professionals fall short is that they understand this intellectually, but experientially and habitually they do not behave in trustworthy ways.

To set ourselves on the right trustworthy path, let's begin by looking at how untrustworthy perceptions are created, reinforced, and fostered. See if you recognize any of these trust-busting traits in others or yourself.

When Working with Clients, to Earn Trust You Should Avoid:

★ Dressing like you're on vacation, a hobo or a hooker.

★ Speaking in shallow generalities (you'll learn how to engage your clients much more deeply, shortly).

★ Demonstrating sloth, ignorance, and apathy.

★ Acting inconsistently.

★ Forgetting to apologize when you've screwed up; making excuses, blaming others.

★ Bragging and broadcasting about yourself: YOU are NUMBER ONE! Talk about YOU exclusively. Talking more than YOU listen.

★ Acting like YOU are the most important person in the room.

★ While on appointments with clients, interrupting what you're doing with them to take phone calls and check e-mail from others.

★ Sprinkling your MLS listing remarks, Internet property promotions, and marketing materials with misspelled, flaccid, and uninspired ad copy.

★ Cutting corners, doing as little as possible and only what's required.

★ Keeping clients in the dark, uninformed and guessing.

★ Following up and responding slowly, at your convenience or not at all.

★ Acting moody, whimsical, lackadaisical, or all three.

★ Having no systems in place so that you are always winging it by the worn seat of your under-pants.

★ Breaking your promises and ignoring your commitments.

★ Running late.

You know, it takes only one or two of these untrustworthy behaviors to alienate us from opportunity. All of them are to be avoided at all costs.

Now that we've reminded ourselves what behaviors to avoid, let's look at which behaviors and actions will help earn us trust and build credibility.

Sixteen Ways to Earn True-Blue Trust and Credibility Trust is earned when we:

★ Treat others with respect and courtesy.

★ Communicate with calm confidence.

★ Listen more than talk.

★ Include facts, details, names, dates, statistics, testimonials, references, and sources. Strive to show, not tell.

* Employ professional-grade tools, systems, techniques, and people.

* Act energetic, enthusiastic, and in the present.

* Take pride in our work, demonstrate commitment, respond promptly, and act professionally.

* Ask lots of questions about what, how and when *they* want it, so we can deliver it *their* way.

* Collaborate, accept responsibility, keep our commitments, and correct our mistakes with a positive attitude.

* Provide a detailed, written marketing plan, including examples, samples, and track record results.

* Keep our clients informed in ways that respect what, how, and when they want their information.

* Lead with a positive attitude, candid conversations, and crisp execution.

* Are consistent in word and deed.

★ Admit when we don't know something and are prepared to find the correct answer, pronto.

★ Allow our clients to fire us on the spot if we break a promise, slack, or suck. No questions asked. No fees. No hassles.

Facing the Trust Challenge Together

I've been in this business for over thirty-two years. During that time, civilian perceptions of our profession haven't budged out of the cellar. If anything, advances in technology and gains in societal savvy have made it easier than ever for all of us to spot and avoid lame sales people. The advent and adoption of Internet ratings systems like Yelp.com, Zillow.com, and social media networks like Facebook mean that wary citizens can now identify, choose, and recommend trustworthy service providers, as well as instantly warn their friends and followers whom to avoid.

For you and me, this is fantastic news. By infusing your business approaches with the trustworthy actions outlined in this book, combined with your excellent personality traits and life experiences, it's easy for you to rise above the vast pack of mediocre real estate agents. Instead of your clients hearing Blah-Blah when you engage with them, they'll think Ah-Ha, this real estate agent is unique, behaves in trustworthy ways, and is choosable. Because of this, the future for you is bright.

Next up: It's one thing for you to know that you're a trustworthy real estate professional. But for that to translate into tangible business for you, other people need to know that too. Which means capitalizing on what savvy marketing people call **Top of the Mind Awareness**. Want to know about that? Read on...

Chapter Four

Make Top of Mind Awareness Work for You

"If you have a talent, use it in every which way possible. Don't hoard it. Don't dole it out like a miser. Spend it lavishly like a millionaire intent on going broke."

~ Brendan Francis, Irish Poet

How Top of Mind Awareness Works

If nobody knows you as a trustworthy, knowledge-able, and remarkable real estate agent, you don't have a chance. You'll starve. Here's why.

Having tracked thousand of transactions throughout my real estate career and scrutinizing the professional research that's available, I can share with confidence that **over 70% of homebuyers and sellers choose a real estate agent they know and trust, or who was referred by a trusted friend.** But don't take my word for it.

One of the most important elements of a trustworthy presentation is to *tell less* and *show more.* Also, using third-party proof, when possible, adds weight and credibility. To that end, let's continue by reviewing these startling revelations from an official source – the National Association of Realtors®. After we review these survey results, we'll dive into what the survey results tell us about what we should and shouldn't be doing, and how we can catapult our business success from starving to well-fed.

2010 National Association of REALTORS® Profile of Home Buyers and Sellers.

Exhibit 7-1	METHOD USED TO FIND REAL ESTATE AGENT
(Percentage Distribution)	
Referred by (or is) a friend, neighbor or relative	41%
Used agent previously to buy or sell a home	23
Personal contact by agent (telephone, email, etc.)	4
Visited an open house and met agent	4
Referred by another real estate or broker	4
Internet Web site	4
Saw contact information on For Sale/Open House sign	3
Referred through employer or relocation company	3
Walked into or called office and agent was on duty	2
Direct mail (newsletter, flyer, postcard, etc.)	2
Newspaper, Yellow pages or home book ad	2
Advertising specialty (calendar, magnet, etc.)	1
Other	6

As we can see from this chart, *referred by (or is) a friend, neighbor, or relative* and *used agent previously* continue to be among the most important factors when choosing a real estate agent.

The chart below identifies which important factors influence which agents they choose to contact and interview.

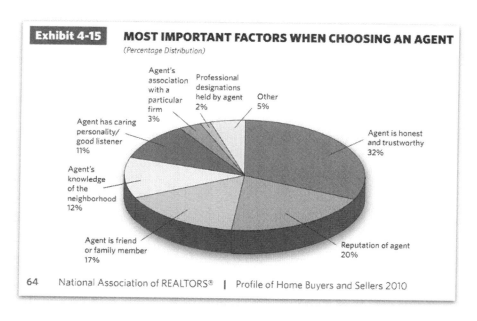

Exhibit 4-15 MOST IMPORTANT FACTORS WHEN CHOOSING AN AGENT
(Percentage Distribution)

Agent's association with a particular firm 3%

Professional designations held by agent 2%

Other 5%

Agent has caring personality/ good listener 11%

Agent is honest and trustworthy 32%

Agent's knowledge of the neighborhood 12%

Agent is friend or family member 17%

Reputation of agent 20%

64   National Association of REALTORS® | Profile of Home Buyers and Sellers 2010

In this chart we learn that *trust, reputation, listening, and market knowledge* play key roles in choosing which agents a homebuyer or seller will contact and interview.

Note that agents with the biggest ads, agents who send the most direct mail, agents who brag the most, and agents who hope the most don't show up as a Most Important Factor.

Now that we have a handle on which agents are chosen and why, the next chart reveals how many agents a motived homebuyer or seller will consider.

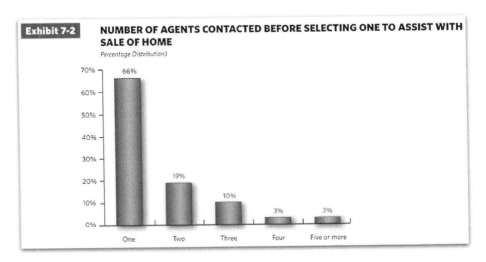

NUMBER OF AGENTS CONTACTED BEFORE SELECTING ONE TO ASSIST WITH SALE OF HOME

Exhibit 7-2

Percentage Distribution)

These three charts make three things brilliantly clear.

1. Seven out of ten sellers choose an agent they know, or one who has been referred to them.

2. Reputation, trustworthiness, and market knowledge are sky-high on the "agent must-have" list.

3. Surprisingly, four out of five sellers choose to contact and interview only one or two agents.

Let's delve deeper into these three important points.

Seven out of ten homebuyers and sellers choose an agent they know, or one who was referred to them.

Wow, right? This is why having a larger network of past and present clients, friends, and acquaintances is not optional; it's mandatory. The quality and size of our network will absolutely determine the size and quality of our success.

Reputation, trustworthiness, and market knowledge are sky-high on the "agent must-have" list.

The people we know, know more than one real estate agent. For example, my market is a suburb of Houston, a master planned community called The Woodlands. We have an adult civilian population of around 68,500 and a local real estate agent population of around 1,100. That's one real estate agent for every sixty-three adults. This doesn't include the roughly around 24,000 Houston Association of REALTORS® who would crawl across cut glass to list or sell a property in The Woodlands. No doubt, most civilians who live in The Woodlands know more than one real estate agent, agreed? It's likely the same in your market – the people you know, they know more than one real estate agent.

The huge Ah-Ha conclusion we can make is this: Agents who keep a low profile (secret agents) are, in effect, invisible. If an agent is invisible, then there is simply no way that the people they know will know anything about their reputation, whether or not they are trustworthy, a mega-watt marketing savant, or a village idiot. Does that make sense?

If you're beginning to get a funny feeling, like maybe you're a secret agent and people don't know how great you are, don't worry. We're going to cover how to go from secret agent to out-loud visible, attractive, choosable, and referrable, very soon.

Surprisingly, four out of five choose to contact and interview only one or two agents.

Gulp! Homebuyers and sellers have an army to choose from. But guess what? They don't consider or interview an army. When needing a real estate professional, four out of five people only choose one or two lucky agents to talk to. That's wow-wild, right?

When civilians have a real estate need, or are asked to recommend a reliable real estate agent, out of *all the agents* they could choose from, most choose to engage with only one. That means that if we aren't the first or second agent they think of, we are completely and utterly screwed. This is why secret agents are starving, stressed, and struggling. Because secret agents are invisible and therefore never thought of, they're never called-on or referred.

Now that we know how civilians behave, what can we do so that when someone we know has a real estate need, shazam, we are the ones who magically pop into their conscious thoughts? Becoming the first or second person they choose to call on isn't magic or luck at all. It's really a combination of science and art called **Top of Mind Awareness**.

How Top of Mind Awareness Works

I'd like you to read each of the following five questions in turn, jotting down your answers or speaking them out loud. Again, please *do* this exercise, don't skip over it. The idea here is to give you an experience of what I'm talking about, not just some dry theory:

1. When I say *to-die-for dessert*, what taste sensation makes your mouth water and your face smile? What dessert did you think of?

2. When someone asks you to name *the greatest rock-n-roll band of all time*, who do your ears hear? Name the band or artist.

3. You've been offered your *favorite cocktail*. What drink do you immediately think of? Let's hear you say it out loud, as you would to the bartender.

4. Now think of a *sexy and romantic vacation destination*. What place comes to mind? Who'd you take? Speak the location and their name.

5. When I ask you to name a *top performing real estate agent* other than yourself, who do you think of?

The answers to all of these questions are examples of **Top of Mind Awareness** in action. Who or what occupies your first recall position in a certain category is the definition of **Top of Mind Awareness**. Your contextual recall category is "real estate agent." In the next chapter we'll dive into the two contextual types of recall, *professional* and *personal*, why they are important, and how you can use them to take more listings and make more sales.

Now here's a $100,000+ a year question. Within your network of acquaintances, friends, neighbors, relatives, and past clients, when they have a real estate need or when they are asked to refer a trustworthy real estate agent, do they think of you first or second, or not at all? Are you benefitting from **Top of Mind Awareness**?

If you are, congratulations. Always keep in mind that your most ambitious and savvy competitors are trying to erase your **Top of Mind Awareness** and replace it with their own. Keep up the good work and stay Top of Mind.

If you need to amplify your **Top of Mind Awareness**, no worries, we're going to talk about how you can do that right now.

Top of Mind Awareness

Creating **Top of Mind Awareness** is a simple concept and has an easy-to-follow formula, but the execution of it takes hard work, diligence, and commitment. The good news is, if you'll engage in that hard work, diligence, and commitment, you'll change everything – big time.

Remember the two keys to success? Knowing what others don't and doing what others won't. Understanding what **Top of Mind Awareness** is and how to benefit from it is a perfect example of knowing what others don't and doing what others won't.

The 3 R's: Relevance. Remarkable. Repetition

To earn righteous recall, you'll need to rain your network with these 3 R's.

Relevance: The most important thing to know about relevance is this. It's not about *you, your* awards, how epic *you* are, how many homes *you've* sold, how *you're* number one, and so on and so on. Why is none of that old-school bragging relevant? Because nobody cares much about you; *everyone cares about themselves and the important people in their lives.* Don't you agree?

So the question is, how do you achieve relevance? By paying attention and observing what others are interested in, want, need, and desire. Listen long and hard – what questions do they need answered? What things make people smile and nod? What problems do people need solved? What information do people value or find interesting?

So, the formula for Relevance is to:

1. Focus on *them* and the important people in their lives, not you.

2. Come to a conclusion or two about what *they're* interested in, need ,or want; what questions need answering, what *they* want to avoid, and what services and solutions you can provide.

3. Share what is relevant.

4. Lather, rinse, repeat.

Remarkable: Average and ordinary is forget-table; remarkable is memorable. If you want to be remarkable you can't walk, talk, chew gum, act, look, work, communicate, or engage in ordinary or expected ways. Many people struggle with the concept of *being remarkable* because they mistake it with somehow being outlandish. Relax, you don't have to be outlandish or a superhuman.

Remarkable simply means *worthy of remark*. It's easy to be worthy of remark if you do the following eleven things sincerely.

1. Show up on time.
2. Listen and pay attention.
3. Deliver as promised.
4. Be consistent.
5. Keep your promises, be generous.
6. Don't brag, complain, or make excuses.
7. Don't push and shove.
8. Follow up.

9. Follow through.
10. Have a sense of humor.
11. Be patient, positive and passionate.
12. _____

13. _____

14. _____

15. _____

Go ahead and fill in blanks 12 – 15 with actions or behaviors you feel would glide you from ordinary to remarkable (you'll notice some strong similarities to the formula for relevance).

See, being remarkable isn't being outlandish: it simply involves showing up, being sincere, and, most of all, behaving in a trustworthy way.

Repetition: This is about consistent and remarkable conduct, contact, conversation, sharing, and engagement. Here's a handy list of old and new school media in which you can rain your remarkable repetition:

★ In Person

★ Telephone/Cell phone

★ Personal Mail (i.e., handwritten)

★ e-mail

★ eNewsletter

★ Twitter.com

---

* Facebook.com

* LinkedIn.com

* Video - Youtube.com

* Blog Posts

* Blog comments

* Texting

* Online Chat

* Advertising

* Direct Mail

Creating indelible **Top of Mind Awareness** is one of the most valuable skills a real estate agent can possess. Master this and you'll easily move from Blah-Blah boring to Ah-Ha attractive and perpetually successful.

What Have We Discovered?

Let's wrap up this chapter with a summary of what we've discovered about what homebuyers and sellers do when they need real estate services:

★ The vast majority of homebuyers and sellers talk to only one or two agents at most before selecting who they will offer their business to.

★ Most civilians typically know more than one real estate agent and have access to hundreds. The one or two real estate agents they call on are contacted because they are already known and trusted, or they were recommended by a trusted friend.

★ When real estate services are needed, if we're not the first or second real estate agent that person thinks of, we're sunk.

To succeed in this business we must create **Top of Mind Awareness** in the memories of everyone we know. We do this through relevant, remarkable, and repetitious contact, engagement, and marketing impressions. As you read further, you'll find that this book is full of high wattage ideas, strategies, and actions that position you in winning form within the minds and memories of your clients, prospects, and suspects.

So far in this section of the book we've determined what business we're *really* in. We've discovered why we need to be in the business of building and maintaining trust with everyone we meet.

And we've looked at the concept of **Top of Mind Awareness** to ensure we're preferably the first or – at worst – the second real estate professional that civilians think of when they need our services. Are you ready to jump into the thick of it, kick ass and take names? Er...not just yet. We're off to a solid start, but there's more to know and do.

There are a few other tips I'd like to share with you. The first of which is how to ensure that the people who know you, or know of you, don't just *know* you. We want them to instantly think of you first and foremost *in the right context.* Here's what I mean...

Chapter Five

It's Not Who You Know, It's Who Knows You

"You are doing all the business you will ever do, based on the number of people who are aware of you now."

~ Steve Rand, Real Estate Broker & Speaker

Popular + Funny + Smart + Sexy + Fun +Caring = So What?

Here's the thing. Sure, it's better to be popular, funny, smart, sexy, caring, and any number of other positive characteristics than it is to be invisible. But in and of themselves, these traits don't ensure our success in the real estate business. While it's true that a larger network of friends, acquaintances, and professional associations are important ingredients in developing a successful business, there's more to it. Much, much more.

Friendship, familiarity, and acquaintance are nice to have, but represent only latent potential. It doesn't matter if we've known someone for umpteen years: our kids play together; or we've partied, cried, laughed, loved, or vacationed together. Just because we know someone and they know us does not mean that when they have a real estate need they'll think to call on us.

To earn invitations to list and sell and to receive plentiful referral recommendations, the people you know have to *perceive you* as a trustworthy and choosable *real estate agent* at least as much, and ideally more, than they perceive you as *anything else*. What I'm saying is, *the context in which people perceive you is key.*

Here's How Contextual Perception and Recollection Works

When we think of the people we know, we tend to think of them in the context of our most frequent, memorable, and relevant interactions. And these interactions can be broken down into two categories: Social Context and Professional Context.

Social Context

When we think of the people we know in a social context, our primary perceptions, and recollections of them revolve around social interactions. Generally we introduce these people in a social context. Whatever their profession, it's shared secondarily or not at all.

For example, here are three social context introductions:

"This is my friend Lani. She and I are in a Bunco group together."

"Meet my friend Laura. She's my daughter's best friend's mother."

"I'd like to introduce you to Bill. He and I play racquetball together at 24-Hour Fitness."

Professional Context

When we think of the people we know in a professional context, our primary perceptions and recollections of them revolve around professional interactions. Generally, we introduce these people in a professional context. Whatever social connections we've had with them, these are shared secondarily or not at all.

For example, here are three professional context introductions:

"This is my friend Lani. She's a real estate attorney with Smith & Simon."

"I'd like you to meet Laura, who's an art dealer. Maybe you've been to her gallery, French Twist?"

"This is Bill. Be sure to mind your manners because he's a K9 cop with the Houston Police Department."

Do you see the difference between the two types of context?

Why Context Matters

As we discussed earlier, we know from surveys, studies, and personal experience that the majority of homebuyers and sellers choose an agent they know and trust, or an agent that was recommended to them by someone they know and trust.

When people need the services of a real estate agent, they call on the first or second agent they think of. If the people you know think of you primarily in a social context, you will not be considered, chosen, or referred. How can they consider, choose, or refer you if they don't immediately think of you as being in the real estate business?

If the people you know think of you primarily in a professional context, then you have a shot at being considered, chosen, or referred. Otherwise, forget it!

The important question you want to ask yourself, and be brutally honest with yourself about, is: "Which context do the I know associate me with?" If the answer is in a social context, you'll want to immediately begin shifting their perceptions toward a professional context. If you believe you already benefit from being perceived in a professional context, the next steps are to reinforce and deepen those perceptions in ways that cause people to think of *you first* when they have a real estate need.

Whatever the status of your **Top of Mind Awareness**, your business will benefit by creating undeniable professional context. Fortunately it's not difficult. Here's how it's done.

Creating Professional Context

It's simple. To be perceived as a trustworthy and choosable real estate professional, all you have to do is behave like one. If you will not only read this book, but also put the philosophies, strategies, activities and actions into play, you will easily, respectfully, effectively and proudly create a professional persona that is attractive, memorable, choosable and referrable.

It doesn't mean slippery-spit how many people we know – or how many people know us. It only matters who knows us in the context of a professional, trustworthy and choosable real estate agent.

The Two Reasons Why Sales Sag

We've already discovered the first reason why people didn't choose you as one of the two real estate professionals they might contact and consider when they have a need: They didn't think of you. More specifically, they didn't think of you in a relevant professional context. In essence, you were invisible to them and missed out. If this is happening, you'll want to get working on that **Top of Mind Awareness**, lickety-split!

The second reason is: YOU didn't know THEY were thinking of selling or buying – you couldn't and didn't pursue or follow up on the opportunity. In essence, the opportunity was invisible to you.

Out-and-about real estate agents collide with opportunity. Some call it being lucky; I believe we create our own luck. Prosperous agents push themselves away from distraction, out of the office, and into the welcoming arms of real-life adventures with real people. They're engaging in *On-Purpose*

---

and *In-Person Conversations*. They're connecting with people around shared passions.

People hire and referral recommend people they like and trust. People like and trust those who are sincerely interested in the same things they are. So let's now take a brief detour into the wacky world of psychographics.

Chapter Six

Why the Future of Your Future Is Psychographic

"Whatever you are, be a good one."

~ Abraham Lincoln

Has this ever happened to you? Weeks of involvement in a new professional group (The Chamber Of Commerce, Rotary, et al) drag by. You're not having any fun. Pouring yourself into it, people don't seem to appreciate you at all. You're likable, but you're not *connecting*. Group members aren't treating you rudely, but relationships aren't blooming. You joined this group to network and share leads, but your efforts are completely barren.

What Went Wrong?

This misfit story unfolds when the decision to join a group, organization, tribe, or niche is based on demographics – or worse, random happenstance. Here's why. Your *passions* are not in alignment with the group you've selected. These people aren't your kind of people, you feel it, and they know it. Ergo, nothing good happens; your efforts remain fruitless.

The fix is simple and quick. *When you engage with a tribe that has shared passions, interests, activities, and opinions, you click and stick.* Clicking and sticking happens when you've joined the right tribe because you're just like them, and in return, they like you.

So how can we be sure to pick the right tribes and connect with y*our kind of people?* Let's learn about what modern marketing savants call psychographics. Whoa! Psychographics sounds like an intimidating name, and some sort of psychobabble bullshit, but it's not. It's being used by iconic brands like Apple, GE, Nike, and Starbucks. Understanding what psychographics is about and how you can use this knowledge to better connect with people and grow your business is simple and powerful.

What's Psychographics Anyway?

Wikipedia.com defines psychographics like this:

In the field of marketing, demographics, opinion research, and social research in general, **psychographic variables** are any attributes relating to personality, values, attitudes, interests, or lifestyles. They are also called IAO variables (for Interests, Activities, and Opinions). They can be contrasted with demographic variables (such as age and gender), behavioral variables (such as usage rate or loyalty), and firmographic variables (such as industry, seniority, and functional area).

See, understanding psychographics is pretty simple; basically you want to hang out with people with *similar interests, shared beliefs,* and in common *passions* and *hobbies.* People with things in common tend to like each other. People are comfortable with and trust people they like. People hire, recommend, and refer people they know, like, and trust. This is why understanding psychographics and these IAO (*Interests, Activities, and Opinions*) variables is important. Now let's take a look at how to put our new knowledge to work.

Psychographic Segmentation

To leverage your efforts, deepen connections, forge stronger relationships, earn trust, and have more fun, it's wise to analyze your SOE (Sphere of Engagement/Sphere of Influence) and segment these individuals into tribes or niches of similar Psychographic makeup.

Here's How:

Step One: Let's begin with some Psychographic Segmentation. Group your Sphere of Engagement (SOE) into tribes and niches with in-common IAO (Interests, Activities, and Opinions) variables. We're doing this because each psychographic tribe has its own language and psychographically imprinted this-is-relevant-and-interesting-to-me hot buttons.

Step Two: When crafting marketing messages, whether they are institutional, personal branding, property promotion, presentation, or prospecting, always speak *their language* and talk mostly, or only, about what interests them. Do this and connection, conversation, persuasion, trust and **Top of Mind Awareness** will take deep root, and your success will bloom brilliantly. You'll have more fun, too.

I started this chapter by sharing a common story. *Real estate agent joins sexy-looking demographic group to meet new people. Agent doesn't connect because the group psychographics don't match. No connection, no fun, no appreciation, no business.*

This sad story happens over and over again. To keep from beating your head against the "*you're not like us*" asphalt wall, consider the Psychographic variables of any group before you join it. When you engage with a tribe that has shared passions, you click and stick.

Here's another important point. Immediately quit mis-picked tribes and scoot into a tribe that is involved in something you're *passionate* about; a tribe with compatible *Interests, Activities and Opinions.*

Do This Now

Speaking of passions, now is the time to open your mind and imagination. What passions singe you? What passions do you think you don't have time for? Cooking classes, yoga, book club, Bunco, ballroom dancing, PTO, tennis league, coaching little league? The real estate business is one of the few businesses that allow positive people opportunities to engage in people-centric passions. Forget about joining the traditional, professional organizations unless you're passionate about them. Join the tribes and niches that you love. They'll love you back. When this happens you and your tribe win. You'll grow trust and discover new opportunities. Have fun, live it up, share, serve and succeed brilliantly. Yea!

And next, a short story about one of your earliest life lesson on how to treat others, The Golden Rule.

Chapter Seven

The Golden Rule 2.0

"Anybody running beats anybody walking, any-body walking beats anybody sitting."

~ Tom Bunk

The Golden Rule 1.0

It was forty-five years ago. I was eight. Our steel chairs were painted shiny brown, my tiny butt was sore from steel sitting, and I was fidgety. Gravelly voiced from smoking, Mr. Lafon read the good word from his worn-familiar Holy Bible. His was the King James Version, the one with red sentences, golden edges and lots of Thee, Thou and Verily words. This Sunday School morning, he shared the Golden Rule:

"Do unto others as you would have done unto you."

I imagine, along the way, some loving person shared the Golden Rule with you too? Wise words to live by; Robyn and I taught this to our own children when they were tykes. But in today's business world, the Golden Rule is broken. In fact, if we conduct our business based on Golden Rule 1.0 principles, we'll go bust.

Now, please don't get all indignant and huffy, hear me out. Let me introduce you to the...**The Golden Rule 2.0**

"Do unto others as <u>THEY</u> would have done unto themselves."

In this 2.0 version, notice the focus is on *them*, not you. Think about that for thirty seconds. Reread it:

"Do unto others as <u>THEY</u> would have done unto themselves."

How do you want to be treated, serviced and tended to? Do you prefer it the way you want it, when you want it, how you want it? The way you like it best?

Or, do you prefer your personal preferences to be sloughed off and overridden in favor of what someone else thinks is best for you? I think we all would rather have what we want, the way we want it, not the way someone else thinks we should have it. Wouldn't you agree? Sloughing off someone's desires and preferences for your own leads to Fail with a capital F.

A Fail Example of What I'm Talking About

Let's say we're friends and we bump into each other at the bar. "Hey, how's it goin'? Great to see you! Let me buy you a drink?", I offer. You smile and nod thirstily. I don't ask, "What'll you have?" Hell no, I just go ahead and order you what I like. I flag the bartender down and ask her to pour you a double Crown Royal on the rocks. Your mouth waters for a flute of crisp Kim Crawford, but now you have a fistful of whisky and your smile is upside down. Ordering for you without asking you would be borderline rude of me, right?

See what I mean? Treating others *as-you-like* instead of *as-THEY-like* can lead to fractures: relationship fractures – the compound kind – with jagged bones poking out.

Treat Others as They Want – Please

This is the easy part. How do you know how others want to be treated? The answer is the same for work, play, and love. **Ask, of course.**

Ask conversational, candid questions about what others want. How they like it and when they want it. Then you give it to 'em, plain and simple. Let's take a look-see at how this could play out on a listing appointment.

Three Don't and Do Examples

Example Number One:

Golden Rule 1.0 = Ms. Seller, **let me tell you** what I'm going to do for you. Others love it. I love it, and it works well for me, I'm a big success, you know. Let me tell you all about it. [Telling and Selfish Selling = Blah-Blah.]

Golden Rule 2.0 = Ms. Seller, what are the three most important things your real estate agent can do for you? What criteria will you use to select your agent? [Asking and Listening = Ah-Ha.]

Example Number Two:

Golden Rule 1.0 = Ms. Seller, you said communication was important. Here's the good news, I'm real good at it. I e-mail a written report every two weeks. I'll touch base every thirty days with an updated market analysis. If you have any questions, call me. I return all my calls within twenty-four hours. Like I said, people say I'm great at staying in touch. [Telling and Selfish Selling.]

Golden Rule 2.0 = Ms. Seller, you shared that communication is important; how would you like to be communicated with, and how often? For example do you prefer phone calls, e-mails, written reports, or _____? To make it convenient for you, what form would you like our communication to take and how often would you like it? [Asking and Listening.]

Example Number Three:

Golden Rule 1.0 = Ms. Seller, you said that Internet marketing is important and you're right. I have fantastic news, I have a website that is as awesome as I am. I'm a web-savvy guru and high-tech is my middle name. I'm even on Facebook and

Twitter. Nobody can do a better Internet job than me. [Telling and Selfish Selling.]

Golden Rule 2.0 = Ms. Seller, you shared that Internet marketing was important. Can you elaborate on that for me? For example, what methods or media, web sites, and types of Internet marketing do you feel are most effective and have the biggest impact? Which ones do you feel are a waste of time? [Asking and Listening.]

You get the picture, right? Here's the bottom line. Before you Gatling Gun ramble and rat-a-tat-tat, tell-tell-tell, and selfish-sell: shut your pie hole, ask questions, listen and learn how *they* want it. Discover what *they* want, expect, desire, and need. Then, simply give it to *them* Golden Rule 2.0 style:

"Do unto others as <u>they</u> would have done unto themselves."

So, What's Next for You?

What questions will you begin asking? What cool things will happen in your business and in your relationships when you start showering *THEM* with what *THEY* like, desire, and want, instead of what you like? You know they will love you for this, right?

End of Chapter – drum roll please.

So far, we've talked quite a bit about who she should be connecting with, the importance of trust, Top of Mind Awareness, and honing our communication skills – now we're going to motor into *where the rubber meets the road* territory. Turn the page, please.

Chapter Eight

On-Purpose and In-Person Contact and Conversations

"You are the only person on earth who can use your ability."

~ M. Kathleen Casey

If you somehow manage to get six hours of sleep, you're left with eighteen mostly awake hours to do all the bajillion things you need to do in the day. Eighteen hours sounds like a lot, but it's not. It's only 1,080 minutes. With your 1,080 minutes you have to take care of yourself, take care of others, make money, run errands, pay bills, love, laugh, cry, play, and plan. Because your time and energy is finite, it's important that your real estate efforts are keenly focused and highly leveraged. You don't have any time to spare, right?

Your Most Important Activity Isn't Hoping

Unfortunately, the real estate business is a hot-bed of hope, and our industry is overloaded with agents who hope that they can advertise, direct mail, and e-mail their way to success. They mistake monologue broadcasting with in-person contact and bombard friends, strangers, and neighbors with postcards and e-cards, hoping for a call back. They shoot out Just Listed and Sold announcements with no personal contact, dreaming of lucky lightning strikes. They spend hours creating the perfect and magically-hypnotic, twelve-page "Why You Should List with Me" expired listing and FSBO seller proposal – then they drop them in the mail and wait for a stranger who doesn't know them to call another stranger (the agent), ask for their help, and throw money at them.

If their direct and e-mail blasting campaign isn't working (and it never does), they double down on hopeless and plunk down maxed-out credit cards to buy worthless magazine and newspaper ads, chasing new strangers…and hoping harder than ever.

Earlier we talked about how buyers and sellers choose their real estate agents – rarely is a stranger chosen. Throughout the book we talk about strategies, tactics, and specifics on knowing what others don't and doing what others won't. All of these ideas are pointless without **On-Purpose and In-Person Contact and Conversations**. Bottom line, without them you can't be successful.

Let's take a look at what happens when **On-Purpose and In-Person Contact and Conversations** happen.

In-Person Contact Leads to Conversations and Connection

In-person contact is the only certain path to success. When contact does not include a conversation, it's not *In-Person Contact*, it's a monologue advertising broadcast. To be clear – direct mail and e-mail blasts, print and electronic advertising, status updates, blog posts, and other forms of online and offline promotions that don't include a conversation do not fall into the *In-Person Contact* category, they fall into the broadcast contact category. (As an aside, there is an important place for strategic and targeted broadcast contact, but it's a supplement to success, not primary to it.)

There are three positive and profitable forms of *In-Person Contact*; I've listed them below in the order of their effectiveness.

1. Face-to-Face – Real Time and Online via Skype, Apple Face Time, Google Chat, etc.

   Face-to-Face is best because we can use all our senses to engage, connect, and communicate. Body language, facial gestures, and tone of voice all add weight and depth to the *conversation,* and meaning to our mutual understanding and connection.

2. Voice-to-Voice – Cell/Telephone

This is second best because we're missing all the visual cues, but we can respond to tone of voice, ask follow up questions to improve our understanding and add context and detail to clarify and colorize our *conversation.*

3. Text-to-Text (virtual) – Social media conversations. Text messaging, online chat, e-mail and other forms of typed conversations.

We've all experienced the conversation-flattening effect of Text-to-Text conversations. When we read another person's dialogue we miss out on important body language, facial gesture, and tone of voice cues. Because we can sometimes misinterpret or misunderstand what's been written, Text-to-Text is at the bottom of this all-important list. But let's not discount the growing importance of this form of *In-Person Contact* by mis-considering it a teenager's toy. Not only are there half a billion people engaging in Text-to-Text conversations on Facebook and other online social media networks, we're sending over 4.1 billion text messages every day. (Let's not ignore, but embrace Text-to-Text, my friends.)

Any way you Ronco Slice & Dice it, the key to success in the real estate business hinges on correct forms of contact. When In-Person Contact is made, conversation takes place, and like bees buzz, possibilities bloom. Especially if one of them *(you)* is listening with elephant-eared interest to what the other person has to say. This is critical because the more sincerely we listen, the better we understand where a person is coming from. The more we understand each other, the more we appreciate each other. When we appreciate each other our **connection** deepens, and our relationships naturally colorize and click as we uncover multiple levels of mutual interest.

Conversation and Connection
Lead to Trust and Discovery

As our connection and mutual understanding grow, so does our trust. Trust leads to sharing our dreams and desires, unmet needs and challenges, likes and dislikes with each other. The more others share with us, the more we discover how we can best help, support, share with, or serve them.

Trust and Discovery Lead to Sharing,
Solving, and Serving

This part is where the rubber meets the road, and is super important. Well, it all is, but this part especially so.

When I speak about **sharing, solving, and serving,** I'm not suggesting you focus exclusively on real estate-related sharing, solving, and service opportunities. In fact, an exclusive focus on real estate things makes us one dimensional and annoying. The goal is to become the *Go-To-Girl/Guy* for all things related to community, family, home, entertainment, lifestyle . . . and real estate stuff.

For example, some of my appreciated sharing has taken place on Facebook and has nothing to do with selling or listing houses. The best conversation starters happen when I talk about everyday life things, when I share personal photos and relevant web links to community information for events, festivals, concerts, and positive local news.

By engaging in one-on-one conversations (on and offline), listening intently and being curiously engaged, you will discover what to share, and how you can help and best serve others.

Aside from the personal examples I shared above, yours might include: recommendations for youth sports leagues for their kids; a housekeeping service; a great (maybe new) local restaurant; the perfect hotel in the city they will be vacationing in next month; the dry cleaner who doesn't break buttons; the lawn maintenance crew that actually shows up when they say they will; the newly released movie you LOVED and thought they would too; an interesting blog post on something they care about. The main point is, share relevant stuff, not just real estate stuff. Your ratio of civilian stuff to real estate stuff should be about 80/20.

When sharing things non-real-estate-related, you never have to mention real estate – simply deliver the information wrapped in your real estate agent wrapper. What do I mean by that? When you e-mail an article, link, or other suggestion, your real estate agent e-mail signature is your wrapper. If you snail mail something, add a couple of business cards; your business stationary and your logo printed on the envelope also double as your real estate agent wrapper. When out and about, during business hours, wear your name badge to remind the people you're talking to what business you're in.

Always follow up your e-mailed or snail-mailed information with a phone call. Simply call them up, say hello, and ask if they received the information you've sent.

Sharing, Solving, and Serving Leads to Being Chosen and Recommended

The beautiful thing about sharing, solving problems, and serving others is that you will find that their appreciation for you, their attraction to you, and their trust and confidence in you grow naturally. Done sincerely, you will tattoo your Technicolor **Top of Mind Awareness** into their subconscious. When they, or their friends, family, neighbors, co-workers, or relatives need information – especially real estate information, solutions, or services – you will be the first person they think of and contact.

Now That We Understand the Importance of In-Person and On-Purpose Contact and Conversations, What Next?

The questions you should ask yourself are:

★ How many In-Person and On-Purpose conversations do I typically have each day?

★ Do I listen with elephant-eared attention?

★ Am I asking the right questions?

★ Am I discovering what others need, desire, enjoy, believe, value, and care about?

★ Do my conversations make others feel significant?

★ Do I share, solve problems, and serve?

If you're not having rich, On-Purpose and In-Person conversations (with civilians, not colleagues) every day, you're strangling your success. If your daily conversations are tainted with aimless yammering, if it's about me-me-me, and blah-blah-yada, you're killing your success and repelling opportunity.

Relationships, financial success, and fun begin and end with personal contact and rich conversations. When you get to Stage III of this book you'll discover dozens of way to create respectful, relevant, and appreciated contact and conversation. Pick a few and get started today; you'll reap the rewards in short order.

Bonus Material

In addition to all the benefits we've just covered, here's another huge bonus. In-Person Conversations position you in the direct-opportunity path of least resistance and convenience. Making these kinds of contacts provides an opportunity for someone to easily and immediately share a referral. You see, people have only 1,080 minutes to get their things done. They're way too busy to stop what they're doing, dial your number, and share a referral. But if *you contact* them, they will happily share an opportunity with you.

Your New Beginning

It's simple. Have more conversations every day. Does this make sense?

Will you have more conversations?

How many In-Person, On-Purpose conversations will you have today?

When will you start?

Let me know how it goes. Rock on!

And Now...

This is the end of Stage I, the part of the book in which we covered the philosophy behind the approach that has helped me and thousands of others' careers go from sour to sweet. So now you're ready to apply The Golden Rule 2.0, establish all-important **Top of Mind Awareness**, identify and connect with compatible tribes by using that psychographic stuff I shared with you, and make In-Person, On-Purpose Contact and Conversations.

No? You're not feel all that King Kong confident yet? Whaddya mean, you have a few extra issues to clear up first? Well, okay...let's deal with them next. Because to be perfectly honest with you, the biggest black-flag barrier to our success is not the economy, lack of experience, your broker...or anything else external. It's those 101 little ways in which we tend to self-sabotage ourselves and our personal success.

Starting with that really big one—FEAR.

STAGE II:

*"If I have lost confidence in myself,
I have the universe against me."*

Ralph Waldo Emerson

Chapter Nine

Are Fear and Doubt Strangling Your Success?

"Fear is the highest fence."

~ Dudley Nichols

If you're human, from time to time this happens. Prickly needles sting your skin from the inside. Salty beads bubble up and bloom from your brow. Your imagination runs rogue; bad things loom dangerous, and your normally wet mouth goes Mojave-dry.

Yes, from time to time, we all experience fear. In the real estate business, fear robs our future—if we let it. Let's take a look at the most common fear factors.

Universal We-Fear Factors

We fear...

- ☹ Rejection.

- ☹ Looking lame, inexperienced, and unworthy.

- ☹ Saying the wrong thing.

- ☹ Awkward interaction.

- ☹ Disapproval from the Get-a-Real-Job police.

- ☹ Not knowing what to do, how to do it, or when to do it.

- ☹ Not knowing the answer. Ugh.

- ☹ Success or Failure.

- ☹ Fill in the blank _____

Fear feelings are normal, but we can't allow them to paralyze and prevent us from engaging in the activities we know will work. In the real estate business, if we don't take action we're dead women walking. So we're between a rock and a hard place, you might say. But the good news is that we can wiggle free from fear. Next, let's look at what scares us. Here are some activities that tend to create paralyzing fear feelings in most real estate agents.

Which Activities Activate Our Fear Feelings?

To make this exercise relevant and real for you, please fill in the blanks:

- Making the in-person prospecting contacts I know I should. *I fear* _____

  _____

- Asking hard, important questions. *I fear*

  _____

- Asking awkward pre-qualifying questions about ability, motivation, and time frame. *I fear*

  _____

- Embracing new methods, technological tools, and social media. I *fear* _____

  _____

- Saying NO. I *fear* _____

  _____

- Scheduling personal time as a priority. *I fear*

  _____

- Maintaining boundaries. *I fear*_____

  _____

- Speaking my mind. I *fear*_____

  _____

For me, what I fear is disapproval, judgment, rejection, lost opportunity, confrontation, looking incompetent, and nobody liking my book. Boo hoo.

Any of the above situations can incite a riot of fearful feelings of rejection, lost opportunities, and looking wildly incompetent. In our real estate business, fear is our natural and mortal enemy, but only when we give fear permission to paralyze us. Counter intuitively; it's also our friend if we approach it right.

If we allow it, fear can become our friend because it signals we're about to leave our comfort zone. When we move outside our comfort zone, we're growing beyond the status quo and above the masses of mediocrity. Another positive aspect of fear: when we confront and conquer our fears, we're jumping through a flaming hoop that the majority of our average and ordinary competitors are either unwilling or incapable of. Woot.

I know, I know. Talk is cheap and it's easier blah-blah-said than ah-ha-done, but consider this approach.

What to Do When We Feel Fearful

Act like Danica Patrick races. You know her, right? Auto racing driver. Placed third in the 2009 Indianapolis 500. Face plastered everywhere on GoDaddy.com. Anyway, back to you acting the way she drives.

So, let me ask you this. Do you drive a car? Through your windshield and down the road, have you witnessed a civilian car crash? Now, either in the flesh, on TV, or YouTube, have you ever seen racecars crash in an explosive spectacle of flame, twisted metal, and car part shrapnel?

Amateur civilian drivers like you and me—we react differently to crashing cars than professional racecar drivers. When rolling-up on a fresh car crash, we react intuitively; professional racecar drivers are taught to respond counter intuitively.

Generally, we respond to our fears like we civilians react to a car crash. Here's what I mean. When we're driving down the road and we see cars crash in front of us, intuitively we slow down, rubber-neck, and cautiously steer our way around the accident. We generally do the same thing when we're fearful: we slow down, stop, or actively try to avoid the thing that scares us.

Professional racecar drivers are taught to respond to crashes counter intuitively. At 187 mph, racecars careen around the track within inches of each other and often scrape paint. When they collide it's not a simple fender-bender – crash shrapnel explodes in every direction, and it's a matter of life or death. Racecar drivers approaching a wreck are taught to hold a steady speed or accelerate and steer their car directly into the center-point of the car crash. Why? Because at 187 mph, if a driver instinctively attempts to steer around the crash, odds are that instead of avoiding the wreckage they'll drive directly into the exploding shrapnel or sideswipe another driver. If they slow down or stop, the speeding cars behind them will rear-end smash into them, causing a horrific chain-reaction, multi-car pile-up.

Professional drivers know the best chance for survival is to feel the fear, face the fear, and take counterintuitive action. Which means they respond as they've been taught: they don't brake or hesitate, they don't swerve or stop, they steer directly into the thing they fear and race forward to Victory Lane.

And so should we.

In real estate, we need to drive our business like Danica Patrick drives her racecar. When we feel fearful, acknowledge it – don't avoid it. Suppress the intuitive desire to hit the brakes and steer around what's scaring us. Instead, like a professional racecar driver, we should respond counter intuitively by speeding forward, directly facing what's scaring us, and taking decisive action.

Will We Always Win by Facing Our Fears?

Sort of.

Let's face it. When we feel the fear and take action anyway, from time to time we're gonna crash and burn, big time. Our metaphorical knees will scrape, our eyes might get blackened, and maybe a pearly white tooth or two will get chipped. At the very least, our pride will sting and our ego will bruise. So what? It won't kill us; it *will* make us more prepared, more experienced, and ultimately, more successful. Here's what Oscar Wilde said about learning from our experiences:

"To regret one's own experiences is to arrest one's own development. To deny one's own experiences is to put a lie into the lips of one's life. It is no less than a denial of the soul."

If we professionally press forward when amateurs brake and swerve, we will win. The saying, *"Fail Faster— Succeed Sooner"* is the perfect mantra for facing, embracing and conquering our fears. Say it with me now, out loud: *I Will Fail Faster to Succeed Sooner.*

Okay, I have a confession. Even now, after all these years in the business, I still murmur this Fail Faster – Succeed Sooner mantra. In the same way that you must prospect for buyers and sellers, as a sales manager, if I don't prospect for talented new team member recruits, I won't succeed, the team won't succeed, and the company won't succeed. That means I have to make In-Person Contact and

On-Purpose Conversations too. When I hear my whiny negative inner voice whisper-warning me of rejection, looking lame and sounding desperate, I suck it up, remind myself that fear is natural, and if I crash and burn it won't kill me, I'll only learn faster. Then I straighten my shoulders, paint a smile on my face, and speed forward to Victory Lane. You can too. Amen.

We Don't Have to Learn All Our Lessons the Hard Way

Professionals train and perfect-practice until they're as good as they can be. *Note: Practice doesn't make perfect, perfect-practice makes perfect. If you practice, drill and rehearse a skill doing wrong things in the wrong order, no matter how hard or how often you practice, you don't get better at the skill, you get better at doing the wrong things in the wrong order. To make practice pay, you have to be doing the right things in the right order. Perfect-practice makes perfect.*

Let me explain to you what I mean by that. Here's another little exercise for you. Do this now:

1. Grab a black ink pen and yellow legal pad.

2. Write down the activities, the situations, and especially the questions and objections that give you the heebie-jeebies in our business. Here are a few of the usual suspects to get you started:

  a. Giving a listing presentation.

  b. Commission cutting, what do you charge, will you take less questions and objections.

  c. "How experienced are you?" questions.

  d. "I don't want to sign your Buyer's Rep Agreement!" statements.

3. One-by-one, create a written response or action plan that will give you the confidence to overcome or eliminate the individual fears you just listed. (More on this in the next chapter.)

4. Diligently train and perfect-practice for a professional outcome. That means feeling the fear, facing directly into it, taking action and learning from the experience.

5. Rinse, lather, repeat.

If you do this, you will prosper. Honestly, you will. Try it and experience your confidence strengthen and your opportunities multiply.

Wait. There's More.

Now let's talk about *self-doubt*, fear's kissing cousin. Self-doubt is the other mean little demon voice that whispers that our bright ideas are dim, our actions are in vain, and success is doubtful. Negative self-talk and self-doubt saws our success off at the knees if we let it.

If you suffer from self-doubt, like I frequently do, here's what our wicked and impish inner voice might whisper and ask:

★ Am I smart enough?

★ Am I old fashioned and out-of-touch?

★ Am I good-looking enough?

★ Am I lazy?

★ Am I boring?

★ Does anyone really care?

★ Does any of this crap really work?

★ Will it last?

★ Am I funny?

★ Do I have any talent?

★ Do people like me?

★ Am I good enough?

I'm self-talking to myself all the time. We all are. When my self-doubt demons speak, I've learned to mask, muffle and most often, slay them. It's not easy and I'm not always successful, but managing my self-talk acts as a powerful energizer, pushing my success and me forward.

Do you self-doubt? If you do, here are thirteen perspectives that help me slay my self-doubt demons. Hopefully, they'll also help you.

Thirteen Ways to Slay Self-Doubt Demons

I begin by listening when my self-doubt demons talk to me. I don't ignore them or self-doubt myself for self-doubting. I don't punish or berate myself. I know that self-doubt is normal and I listen and learn, reminding myself…

1. I'm learning you can't make a cat bark. (Think about that, and how it applies to people and their behaviors.)

2. I'm learning I can't control outcomes that involve other people; I can only control my own actions.

3. I'm learning that when I miss my mark, I can *choose* to mope, blame, and make excuses, or I can *choose* to learn, adjust – and, if it's important – redirect my efforts.

4. I'm learning Lincoln: "*You can please some of the people all the time and you can please all the people some of the time, but you can't please all the people all the time.*"

5. I'm learning to discern the difference between what's sincerely important to me and what I've been conditioned to think others think *should* be important to me. I'm choosing *sincere* over *should*.

6. I'm learning that some days are just crappy days. That's life. Tomorrow's a new day.

7. I'm learning that performance, weather, seasons, and life all ebb and flow, like Costa Rican waves. You can't tame the waves, but you can learn to surf them. Sometimes you catch the waves and ride, sometimes they catch and tool you. The important thing is to paddle back out and catch the next one.

8. I'm learning life is not a sprint and nothing is ever over until I decide it's time to quit. (Sometimes it's important and wise to quit.)

9. I'm learning that letting go means letting go, not sorta letting go, or carrying it lightly. Letting go means releasing it, whatever *it* is.

10. I'm learning to recognize haters, users, and posers—and to avoid and ignore them.

11. I'm learning to enjoy *the now* more.

12. I'm learning that my self-worth is not determined by others, but by myself.

13. I'm learning that if I open my eyes, my ears, and my mind, my self-doubting demons can illuminate opportunities for improvement.

Take Swift, Confident Action

The next time you hear self-doubt whispering trash in your ear, will you talk back and take action? When fear feelings slap you in the face, will you turn the other cheek or take swift confident action, slay your self-doubt demons, and win the success you deserve?

Now that we've kicked self-doubt's ass, our fear feelings are in check, and we're racing forward, in the next chapter let's revisit the subject of perfect practice and the power of preparation.

Chapter Ten

Are You Prepared to Reap
While Sluggards Sleep?

*"Spectacular achievement is always preceded by
unspectacular preparation."*

~ Robert Schuller

Every day, no matter the location and market conditions, people choose a real estate agent and properties are listed and sold. When the market is lush with green grass and low-hanging fruit, even the lazy and unprepared reap oodles of opportunities. When the market is drought-dry, opportunities are scarce, and civilian expectations are lofty, only the poised and prepared plow deep and succeed.

In any real estate market, especially a challenging market, when an opportunity presents itself, victory favors the prepared.

Questions Are Opportunities.

Because you're cool, attractive, hard-working and perceived as trustworthy, people are going to ask you real estate questions.

Some of the questions will be asked in a casual setting and spur of the moment; others will be deliberate and direct, like questions asked on a listing appointment. Whether casual or deliberate, for the prepared, these questions provide conversational opportunities to outshine the average and unprepared and demonstrate your value.

The key to turning conversational opportunities into business opportunities and commission checks is knowing how to confidently, accurately, and attractively answer question(s).

Simply stated, preparation is the difference between an unpaid amateur and a paid professional. If you'd like to become a well-paid professional ask yourself this question.

Am I PREPARED to Answer *Their* Questions in a Relaxed, Confident, Persuasive, and Attractive Way?

Your future in this business is sealed by your Yes or No answer. Specifically, the more prepared and perfect your conversations, the greater your success, even in tough times. Bottom line: to fly high, you must know what you're going to say BEFORE you say it. You must be *prepared*.

About now, you may be thinking that being prepared and knowing what you're going to say BEFORE you say it sounds like I'm promoting scripts – and you detest scripts. Let me assure you, I understand "script-aversion," and I know that nobody, including you and me, will sit still if we feel our ears are being stuffed with canned-cornpone. I get it.

B.U.T

Behold the Underlying Truth: we both know that the highest paid speakers, communicators, connecters, entertainers, and presenters all have one thing in common. Even geniuses prepare, perfect-practice, drill, and rehearse. That's why what they do looks impressively effortless. They know exactly what they're going to say and do, before they say and do it. Do we?

Let's face it, everyone knows the difference between professionally polished and awkwardly amateurish, when they see it. We don't hire or recommend the awkwardly amateurish, and neither will they.

The question we have to ask ourselves is this. . .

Are We Perfectly Prepared to Answer Commonly Asked Questions?

There's a laundry list of questions commonly asked by homebuyers and sellers, before and during the transaction. These questions are asked with different words, but the concerns that spark them are similar.

The average and ordinary agent will answer commonly asked questions lazily. Their answers are routine, impatient, uncertain, nervous, and stuttered in an uninspiring fashion.

High-paid professional answer commonly asked questions as if it's the first time they've heard them, and they are the most important questions of the century. Because they practiced delivering their answers before they're asked, their delivery is received as confident, persuasive, informed, and professional. When people feel their important questions are being answered effectively, they relax and move forward.

For example here are eight questions we must be prepared to answer in a relaxed, confident, persuasive, and attractive way:

1. How's the real estate market? (More on this in Chapter Twelve)

2. Is now a good time to buy?

3. Have home prices bottomed?

4. Will mortgage rates rise?

5. What are mortgage interest rates these days?

6. What commission do you charge?

7. Should I sell now? Is it a good time?

8. How hard is it to qualify for a loan?

Here's A Simple Nine-Point Preparation Plan:

1. Sit quietly and think about these questions.

2. Think hard. Harder than that.

3. Craft an answer, or two, or three, that you can be proud of.

4. Write your answers out. Stephen King said this in his book *On Writing,* published by Simon & Schuster, Inc. 2000.

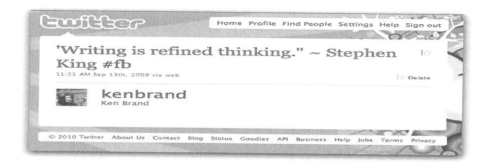

5. Record (use your smart phone to audio or video record) your response. Review, re-craft, record, review, rinse, lather, and repeat, until you feel conversational, relaxed, and confident.

6. Go meet people (In Real Life), connect, and engage.

7. Wait for it. Here it comes. The question you've prepared for.

8. Smile, relax, shine, impress.

9. Rinse, lather, and repeat, for all common moments-of-truth-type questions.

Are You Thinking This Is Too Much Trouble?

Well, you're half right. It's definitely extra effort to do this, and because one of the secrets of success is **"Doing what other's won't,"** this extra effort

---

will set your new standard for excellence higher than the average and ordinary are willing to climb.

Like I said, the level of our preparation seals our futures. It's a natural law: if you want to reap deep while sluggards sleep, be perfectly prepared to answer questions.

Now that we understand the importance of preparation, in the next chapter I'll go into detail about how to take your question-answering skills to even higher levels. The more effective you are at answering big and small questions, the better you'll perform, which leads to more success.

Chapter Eleven

Q&A Self-Sabotage, or Client-Centric Communication?

"Who speaks, sows. Who listens, reaps."

~ *Argentine Proverb*

They meet. Sam and Ella share their important concerns and ask questions. Before the last syllable leaves their lips, in know-it-all fashion Tony gushes and spews his one-size-fits-all answers. Sure, their words entered his ear holes—he heard their words, but he wasn't really listening, so he doesn't precisely understand what they were *really* saying. In his haste to impress and progress, he didn't invest the care or time to pause and ask thoughtful follow-up questions. As a result, he failed to grasp the core essence of Sam and Ella's important-to-them questions and concerns: what they truly want, expect, or need, or what they fear and want to avoid.

This form of self-sabotage is all too common. When we don't understand the true essence of our clients' important-to-them questions, we fail them. By not asking the right follow-up questions, we're self-sabotaging our own success. Even worse, we're doing our clients a disservice – Fail!!

Overestimating and Underestimating

I don't want to suggest that this happens all the time with all of us, but it happens enough times for it to be worrisome. We *overestimate* what we think we know and *underestimate* what we don't know. In our business, we hear the same sort of questions dozens if not hundreds of times. When we hear a familiar question, in a rush to impress and progress, there's a tendency to answer the question, or address the concern based on our previous positive experiences with other people. This is a big problem.

Why?

Because, while each person's questions and concerns may be similar in circumstance, the reality is that these questions and concerns are based on *their* unique personal experiences, expectations, fears, and desires. Sure, we've heard and answered similar questions over and over again, but it's *their* first time asking us these questions, and their circumstances and perspectives are unique to them. The core essence of each client's questions and concerns–or what they truly want, expect, or need – is different, even when on the surface it appears that they are not. So, when our answers and solutions are generic and sized to fit all, the odds of them hitting *their* target, earning *their* trust, and making *them* happy, are razor-slim. Not only is this a disservice to our clients, we're also self-sabotaging our success.

Thankfully, this form of self-spoken-sabotage and disservice can be easily fixed. When our exchange of questions and answers (Q&A) is thoughtful and thorough, understanding is strong, trust is earned, and our clients are served as they wish to be. Remember the Golden Rule 2.0 from Chapter Seven, *"Do unto others as they would have done unto themselves"*? If we keep that in mind we'll stay on course and everyone goes, "Yay."

Let's take a look at what *wrong* and *right* sound like. Imagine overhearing this lame exchange at an important listing appointment. In attendance were two highly motivated sellers and Tony, an unskilled agent.

Listing Appointment – Scenario#1 – The Lame Exchange

Motivated Sellers: Our last agent never stayed in touch. We'd like regular communication. How often will you report to us?

Unskilled Agent: I communicate with all my clients on a weekly basis, I mail a monthly follow-up report, and I e-mail a bi-weekly showing report. All my clients love this; I run a market-activity-update every three weeks. I'm available 24/7, you can call me anytime, yak-yak, blah-blah, yada-yada.

At first blush, it sounds like Tony's keep-'em-in-the-loop communication and stay-in-touch program is pretty snazzy, right? He's sharing what *he believes* is a fantastic follow-up and communication strategy. His last client loved it and *he thinks* it's better than what the other agents in his office are doing. It doesn't really sound like a lame exchange at all, does it? But it is. Here's why.

What he doesn't know—because he's never asked—is his *client's* definition of regular communication and follow-up. Or what they *think* fantastic looks and feels like. He doesn't know *their* preferred frequency, which method of delivery *they* prefer (phone, in person, mail, e-mail, text, etc.), or what specific types of information *they* want. He doesn't know diddly-squat about their specific expectations, concerns, or desires. All he knows is that they said *they* want regular communication and follow-up.

Yes, there's a snowball's chance that Tony's generic answer might satisfy his clients' needs, but what if Sam and Ella's expectations are completely different, or even slightly different? Earlier in this book we learned that the vast majority of sellers and buyers contact two agents. What if the other agent listens and understands just slightly or miles more about Sam and Ella's expectations, wants, and needs? In this instance, Tony wouldn't just have shot himself in his right foot, he would have blown both feet completely off, along with an opportunity to take a salable listing. Equal bummer, Tony will have lost potential sign calls, Internet leads, repeat business, and referral recommendations as well.

What would happen if, instead of rushing to proudly answer, he asked a few clarifying questions instead? Let's find out.

Listing Appointment – Scenario #2 – Crystal-Clear Client-Centric Conversation

Motivated Sellers: Our last agent never stayed in touch. We'd like regular communication. How often will you report to us?

Skilled Agent: Sorry to hear that, Ella. Regular communication can mean different things to different people and I want to make sure I'm delivering precisely what you want. So I'd like to ask a couple of questions. Would that be okay? [Waits for seller's approval].

When you say "regular communication," can we nail down what that looks like for you? For instance, how often would you like an update, what kind of information is important to you, and in what form? I can get you whatever you need—recent market activity, showing agent feedback, marketing activity, things like that—and report back to you by phone, e-mail, snail mail, in person, or however you prefer it. Let's talk about how you'd like to be kept in the loop.

Motivated Sellers: Wow, Tony! You're really different from our last agent; you really listen and ask questions to understand what we want.
You must have read that really awesome book: Less Blah-Blah, More Ah-Ha. We love you and we'll

sign right now. Plus, we're going to pay you a big fat juicy bonus. Plus-plus and super-plus, we're gonna send you a neverending stream of qualified buyers and seller referrals!

Okay, I was just having fun with that last paragraph. The point is, if we put ourselves in the seat of the seller, we can understand how asking thoughtful and thorough questions will lead to crystal-clear and precise communication, which leads to delighted and loyal clients. On top of all that, you'll feel good and proud of how you do what you do.

Be sure to ask thoughtful and thorough questions, before you answer your clients' questions, even if you've heard them dozens or hundreds of times before. To help keep you on track, here's a simple four-step Crystal-Clear Communication model for answering questions effectively.

Step One: **Gain Understanding and Clarity**

Step Two: **Confirm Mutual Understanding**

Step Three: **Share Your Answer/Solution**

Step Four: **Achieve Agreement**

Step One: Gain Understanding and Clarity

After the question is asked, smile, breathe, and relax. To identify, clarify, and understand the true essence of their question(s) or concern(s), ask follow-up questions, such as:

I appreciate how you feel, please tell me more about. . .

Could you please elaborate on that. . .

Can you describe how/when . . .

You get the picture, right? Ask your follow-up questions in a conversational tone with a relaxed body posture. By taking the time to really understand your clients' needs, desires and fears, you're providing a positive and powerful service to them and to yourself. Enjoy the interaction adventure and smile.

Step Two: Confirm Mutual Understanding

When you're finished asking your follow-up questions, confirm that your understanding matches the true essence of their questions or concerns, by feeding this back and asking if you are on track. If they say yes, congratulations – you understand them perfectly. But before we move to the next step, I want you to ask if there's anything else they are concerned about. If there is, listen, and repeat Step One.

Continuing the client-centric listing appointment scenario, Step Two – Confirm Mutual Understanding – might sound like this:

Skilled Agent: Thanks. Let's see if I understand what's important to you. Your last agent didn't follow up or communicate effectively. What you'd like is a weekly telephone call, and I heard you say Wednesday evening would be best. You'd also like a weekly e-mail summary showing appointment feedback, marketing effort updates, and any new market activity in your neighborhood. Ella, you'd like to be the point of contact; Sam, my man, you'd like to be copied in on the e-mail update. Does that sum it up?

Motivated Seller: Yes.

Skilled Agent: Is there anything else about my communication or follow-up with you that we haven't covered, but is important to you? I don't want to miss anything.

Motivated Seller: Nope, you've got it. Thanks for really listening.

Asking follow up questions and confirming that your understanding is crystal-clear and matches the true essence of their questions and concerns is universally appreciated. It also demonstrates your keen interest in what's important to *them*. This approach easily separates you from the unskilled masses. Everyone wins when you use this Four-Step Model. It works like magic in business, and all your other relationships too. Give it try.

Now that we've confirmed we understand our clients' questions and concerns, we move to Step Three, which is where we share our answers/solutions.

Step Three: Share Your Answers/Solutions

When we ask appropriate follow-up questions and the client confirms our crystal-clear understanding, we know exactly what's important to them. In essence, our client has shared *exactly what they are looking for.* All we have to do at this point is share our tailored to *exactly match what they're looking for* answers and solutions. Of course, as always, relax, smile, and share your answers in a conversational and confident manner.

Here's an example:

Skilled Agent: Per your expectations and preferences, I'll report to you weekly by phone, Wednesday evening, between 7 p.m and 8 p.m. We'll discuss anything important to you, showing appointment feedback, a marketing campaign update, and any new market activity in your neighborhood. Ella, you'll be the primary point of contact, and Sam, I'll be sure to cc you on the e-mail updates.

Follow these three Steps, and then finish strong by moving to Step Four.

Step Four: Gain Agreement

This step will sound duh-obvious, but the unskilled leave it out because they haven't read this book and/ or they fear a negative response. Traditional sales education teaches us that salespeople need to *close* and *ask for the order.* I like to think of *the close* and *asking for the order* as simply asking if *their* needs have been met, are they happy, and if we have their agreement to move forward. By asking if our answers and solutions are on the mark, we're doing what others call *closing* and you and I will call *gaining agreement* and *permission to move forward.*

Here's an example:

Skilled Agent: I think I've covered all the important points. Do you both feel that I've answered your questions and addressed your communication and follow-up concerns in a fully satisfactory way?

Motivated Sellers: Yeah, it sounds good, dude.

Skilled Agent: Great. Then as far as my communication and follow-up commitment are concerned, we're in agreement. Let's move forward.

The Take Away

What positive impact would you and your clients experience, if both of you were dancing in perfect communication rhythm? This crystal-clear and client-centric Four Step Q&A model works equally well with clients, prospects, lovers, significant others, and co-workers. In fact, it works with all humans. Use this four-step strategy and you're on your way to real estate rock star status, raving fans, more listings, more sales, and fewer problems and misunderstandings.

As great as all this sounds, you'll do even better (yes, it really is possible) when you become a consummate storyteller. Find out how, next.

Chapter Twelve

Are You Seizing Hiding-in-Plain-Sight Opportunities?

"It is a puzzling thing. The truth knocks on our door and we say, 'Go away, I'm looking for the truth,' and so it goes away. Puzzling."

~ Robert M. Pirsig, Zen and the Art of Motorcycle Maintenance

Have you ever searched high, low, and sideways for your missing reading glasses, only to realize you were wearing them? Have you ever scampered up and down the stairs, searching and mumbling about your lost car keys, only to discover they've been in your right pocket all along? Gah! Don't you want to slap yourself in the forehead when this happens?

Okay, I'm going to share another daily forehead-slapping situation. This happens to real estate agents, usually more than once a day. Here it is.

Profitable Business Opportunities
Found Hiding in Plain Sight

Scads of time and money is burned chasing strangers and scampering after suspects and fool's-gold leads. We chase high, low, and sideways for listing and selling opportunities. All the while, a parade of friends who know us, like us, and trust us—the kind of friends that would happily choose and recommend us—are standing right in front of us. But, like our allegedly lost eyewear and car keys, we don't see them. These golden opportunities are hiding in plain sight and occur when our friends ask, *"How's the real estate market?"*

Let me ask you: How many times a day are you asked some variation of the question, *"How's the real estate market?"*

I posed this very question in a recent sales meeting. Our icon team members reported being asked this question, on average, twice a day. What's your average? If you're new to the business, your number may be less; if you've been around a while, maybe it's higher. Either way, opportunities present themselves every time this question is asked.

Let's say you're asked this question twice a day, five times a week, fifty weeks a year. *That'd be five hundred times a year someone asks you about your business or the real estate market.* Answering this common question uncommonly could be your most profitable *free* golden opportunity. All you have to do to seize this opportunity is be yourself and say the right things, at the right time, in the right way.

Let me show you why this is important and how to do it. Beginning with a little detour into what I call **The Three-People Principle.**

The Mysterious Magic of Three

What comes in threes?

- Genie Wishes
- Goldilocks' Bears
- Alexander Dumas' Musketeers
- Blind Mice
- Stooges
- Jack's (as in Beanstalk) Magic Beans
- A complicated love affair – the French call it *ménage à trois*
- Mind, body, spirit

- Lights, camera, action
- Of the people, by the people, for the people
- Blood, sweat, and tears
- Shake, rattle, and roll
- Add your own here:_____

The list goes on and on and on.

It's Not Scientifically Proven, but. . .

It is evident. Magical energy dances with things in threes. The magical number three dances with real estate agents too. Do you have a pair of comfortable shoes? Slip them on and let's move to the dance floor.

What is The Three-People Principle?

It's that most everyone you know, knows three people who will move in the next twelve months.

Now, do this and see **The Three-People Principle** in action. Walk to your car. Get in. Fasten your seat belt. Start your car. Drive to your bank. Withdraw three crisp Franklins.

Drive to your nearest Starbucks. Lock your car. Walk inside. Approach anyone. Pull out your three crisp $100 bills. Smile. Say, "I will give you $100 for the name of each person you personally know who sold or bought a house in the last twelve months. It can be a coworker, friend or neighbor, someone from church, Bunco, yoga...anyone you know by name."

Smile, listen, and hand over the moola.

Odds are, you'll leave Starbucks with a latte, an empty wallet, and an Ah-Ha belief in **The Three-People Principle**.

So let me ask you, do you believe that most people know three people who have moved in the last twelve months? If you do, then like Jack's three magic beans, let's turn **The Three-People Principle** into a sky-climbing money vine and crowds of new clients.

Here's the deal. We've talked about this before. Most agents wrongly focus their prospecting energy primarily on the question, *"Who in my sphere/network/tribe/niche is going to buy or sell soon?"* This approach is like stepping over dollar bills to pick up dimes. It's the wrong mindset, and has limited opportunity for positive returns.

Here's why.

Statistically, people move every seven to twelve years. Out of 100 people, on average, maybe seven or eight of these 100 folks will make a move during the year. Let's assume you're doing a good job and the 100 fine folks you know like you and trust you. Let's also assume you touch base consistently, meaning you have routine On-Purpose and In-Person conversations with most of them. Of the possible movers, how many of them can you reasonably expect to choose you to list and sell? Five out of eight would be fantastic; probably fewer is realistic, right? So, if you know 100 people, with luck, skill, and strategy, you might be hired three to five times in a year. You can't survive, let alone thrive, on that number, can you? And for those of you with fewer than 100 people in your network – well, the number of opportunities is Olive Oyl skinny, right?

However, by refocusing your mind's eye and your good intentions on **The Three-People Principle**, you will comfortably and dramatically grow your profit possibilities, because your 100 know 300 who will make a move in the next twelve months. Even better, if you're having In-Person, On-Purpose contacts and conversations with 200 people, they know 600 others. If you know 300, they know 900, and so on. Holy mackerel!

Exercise Alert!!

Before we move on, let's make this real. Let's take a look at what your personal golden opportunity is by completing this next exercise. Grab a pen or a pencil and fill in the blanks. It's okay, go ahead and write in this if you want. (In fact, if you aren't already, I encourage you write notes in the margins, highlight key points, and dog ear pages you want to return to later. If you're reading this in an eReader, use all those fancy features to help you remember and return to the material you feel is important.) Fill in the blanks. Don't overthink it, simply use the SWAG (Sophisticated Wild Ass Guess) Method. It doesn't have to be exact, I just want you to get a feel for your total opportunity.

Opportunity Formula Worksheet

Jot down the number of people in each category who live in your market area and would know who you are if you called them and said "hello."

_____ Relatives You Still Speak to

_____ Neighbors

_____ Your Sphere of Influence (When you pick up the phone, dial their number and say, "Hi, <u>friend's name,</u> this is <u>your name</u> calling.", they would know who you are. They wouldn't ask "Who are you?" or hang up.)

_____ People You Know Through Your Significant Others (spouse, lovers, partners, kids, relatives, etc.)

_____ Past Clients

_____ Current Prospects, Suspects and the Curious

_____ Enter the Total Here

X 3

_____ Enter Your Total Here.

This represents the number of people you have both direct and indirect contact with, who will move in the next twelve months.

What Number Of Listing and Selling Opportunities Do You Have?

Can you see how there's a Fort Knox of opportunity associated with people you know directly?

Let me pause here and say this. When I share this exercise in a workshop session, there are always agents who worry that their number of opportunities is limited because their network is skinny. I encourage them, as I do you if you feel this way – No Worries. The primary point is that going forward you understand and use **The Three-People Principle** to build a successful business. In Stage III of this book we cover over a over a dozen individual activities and actions that will add droves of new friends, prospects, suspects, and clients to your network. Relax, no worries. Read on and reap.

But before you move forward and begin to put these ideas and strategies to work, here are a few pointers.

Don't drop friendly, good people to chase strangers.

Do stay in On-Purpose and In-Person close touch with everyone you know. Even when you know that your *friendly, good people** won't move in this century, remember that they will know three people who are likely to move. Build trust, create **Top of Mind Awareness,** and earn the opportunity to politely, professionally, and consistently ask for referrals. They'll gladly give them to you, if you ask.

*Note: I italicized *friendly, good people* because I see too many agents accepting mental and verbal beatings from rude, mean, and unappreciative people. It's important to draw your boundaries around how you will and how you refuse to be treated. When someone you're working with won't respect you, you should fire them and move on. I know the fear of lost opportunity is a powerful thing, but in the long run, even when you win the battle, you lose the war, along with your self-respect. By using the ideas and strategies in this book you will be able to attract and discover so many opportunities, you'll be sitting in the catbird seat and can pick and choose whom to work with. Won't it be nice to work exclusively with nice people? Let's continue...

Don't randomly ask people in your sphere/network/tribe/niche when they are going to move. This is awkward for you and supremely annoying to them. All you need to do is relax and treat your relationships like important relationships, not like transactions. Because you're engaged in frequent, relevant, In-Person contact and conversations, and you're going to put some of these new strategies you're reading about into action, you'll discover and attract these opportunities naturally.

It's that simple.

Reminder: Your mortgage friend knows three, your all-smiles title rep knows three, your grass-stained landscape artist knows three, your sweaty and stern personal trainer knows three, your I-can-fix-anything repair women and men know three, your home stager knows three, your pro photographer knows three, your how-can-I-make-you-shine administrative manager (you don't call them an assistant do you?) also knows three. You get the picture, right?

So, back to the reason why I introduced **The Three-People Principle** to you here in the Seizing Hiding-in-Plain-Sight Opportunities chapter. Everyone who asks you, *"How's the real estate market?"* all know three people who will move within the next twelve months. Maybe one of their friends will hire a real estate agent this week or next. Wouldn't you like to know about that opportunity? Read on to learn how the mediocre miss these opportunities and why you won't.

Turning Blue Sky Opportunity into Real-Life Reality

The mediocre miss these opportunities because they blurt Blah-Blah and cheese-ball common responses to the question, *"How's the real estate market?"* I think this mostly happens for two reasons: they don't understand the opportunity, and/

or, they've never paused long enough to think it through and create an interesting, evocative, or productive answer.

Let's break it down and turn it around.

How Does Cheese-Ball Happen, and What Does It Sound Like?

Forgettable and cheese-ball happens when the answer to the question, **"How's the real estate market?"** is unplanned, unrehearsed, and flaccid. Here are five quick examples of what I'm talking about:

Q: How's the real estate market?

A: *Business is great!" [Yawn. American cheese-ball]*

A: *"I'm really busy." [Boooorrrriinnngggg! Velveeta cheese-ball]*

A: *"The market's picking up." [Sure it is. Roquefort cheese-ball .]*

A: *"Unbelievable." [Whatever. Cheeze-Whiz cheese-ball.]*

A: *"It's slow." [Loser. Goat cheese-ball]*

After any mundane exchange like those above, absolutely nothing good happens for anyone. If you're hyper-rushed, these puny sound bites might be all you can Munster. Any other time, they're lame. Sorry. Don't hate, I'm shootin' straight and sharing solutions.

Will You Work to Become Memorable, Profitable and Cheese-Free?

Memorable happens when our answer to "*How's the real estate market*?" is artfully crafted, interesting, and unexpected. Memorable happens when we know what we're going to say before we say it. Memorable also leads to **Top of Mind Awareness,** which, in turn, leads to being chosen and getting referred. So let's get memorable and turn those **Three-People Principle** possibilities into a bonfire of real listing and selling opportunities. Which means we have to create a new habit of answering this question with an engaging, super-duper-fast short story – instead of cheese ball common.

Super-Duper-Fast and Hyper-Tiny Storytelling

I see you scratching your head, thinking, *When someone asks a simple question, I don't have time to tell a story, even if it's tiny one.* I know. But hear me out. I'm talking hyper-tiny and fast. There's even a formula for it. Using this formula allows us to tap into natural human desires to help others. With an artfully delivered answer to "*How's the real estate market*?", we can engage the attention of our

listeners, naturally and comfortably uncover listing and selling opportunities, and make ourselves
uniquely choosable in the process. Here's how it's
done. . .

Engaging Super-Fast and Hyper-Tiny Stories Have Three Parts

First I'll share what the three parts are, then I'll
share three examples. Aren't you just loving the
number three by now, by the way?

1. **Problems and Benefits** engage the interest of
   the listener. People like to help their friends.
   Whether you ask for it or not, doesn't everyone want to give you advice when you share
   a problem?

   Plus, good people like to share beneficial
   stuff with their friends as well. It's what we
   call word-of-mouth; we all do it when we tell
   our friends about an epic movie, an awesome
   restaurant experience, and cool stuff, people,
   or places we've discovered.

2. **Details and Information** add context and
   believability to a story. If you share a fuzzy
   problem or a fact-free benefit, the story
   sounds suspiciously fiction and BS salesy.
   To sharpen credibility, your story needs to

include specific and vivid details and facts like names, dates, and addresses.

3. **Request for Advice or Help** is how you conclude your super-duper-fast and hyper-tiny story. After sharing details and factual information about the problems or benefits swirling inside your story, you give the listener a chance to do what comes naturally – the desire to help. To do this, we simply ask the listener for help and advice about how to solve our problem, or who they might know who would benefit from our benefits.

Sounds weird and uncommon, doesn't it? It's certainly different from bleating forgettable. And that, my friends, is the sharp point of this chapter.

Let me share a few example answers to the question, "How's the real estate market?"

In these Question and Answer examples, **I'll use bold text to identify Problems and Benefits.** *I'll use italics to identity Details and Information.* <u>And I'll underline text to identify Request for Advice or Help.</u>

Question: How's the real estate market?

Example Answer #1: Thankfully I'm super-busy, but also **frustrated**. I'm working with the nicest couple from *San Diego, Marty and Sarah; she's a chemical engineer with Anadarko, here in The Woodlands.* Anyway, ***I've shown them***

twenty-seven houses and they've fallen in love with the *Clover Park neighborhood, over in The Village of Panther Creek.* **The problem is, there are only four homes for sale and none of them have the three-car garage and greenbelt lot they want. I'm going to have to knock on some doors and see if anyone is thinking of selling.** <u>You wouldn't happen to know of anyone who lives in Clover Park, and is thinking of selling would you?</u> *Marty and Sarah are prequalified, and super motivated.*

Example Answer #2: I feel like I'm running around with my hair on fire, but it's a good thing. I'm holding an *open house this Sunday at a pretty cool house on a cul-de-sac, with a giant lush back yard and a 20,000 gallon salt-water swimming pool.* I'm running around, sending out invitations, coordinating the Internet broadcast, and stuff like that. <u>If you or anyone you know</u> plans to be in the *Clover Park on Sunday, between 2 and 4*, <u>stop in, and say Hi</u>. I'll e-mail you an invitation.

Example Answer #3: Things are great, thanks for asking. *Last Tuesday* I had the most pleasant closing; they really know what they're doing at *Stewart Title.* I was working with the nicest couple from *San Diego, Marty and Sarah.* **We looked at twenty-seven properties and I thought we'd never find their dream home.** Then I was asking around, and a friend – do you know *Theresa Wilson? She's one of the yoga instructors at Villa Sport, she teaches the 5:30 afternoon class on Tuesdays and Thursdays?* Well, last month Theresa referred me to a friend she knew who lived in the *Clover Park neighborhood* and was thinking of selling. Just like that, we showed their home over on *Teal Briar*, they fell in love, wrote a contract, and *moved in Tuesday afternoon.* Now that they're taken care of, **I'm focused on generating some new business.** <u>If you know anyone who needs real estate help, keep me in mind.</u>

As you can see in these three examples, telling a hyper-tiny, super-fast story isn't difficult. The trick to it isn't a trick at all. The key is knowing what you're going to say before you say it. Because you know you're going to be asked this question every day, have your answers ready before it's asked. If you know what you're going to say, you'll answer the question conversationally and confidently. As a result, you attract and discover listing and selling opportunities that were previously hiding in plain sight. Plus, you'll sound remarkably more interesting than all those mediocre agents bleating forgettable.

To help expand your thinking about what hyper-short stories you might share, here are some common situations that you can use for your own super-duper-fast storytelling.

- ✓ Your new listing

- ✓ Your recent closing

- ✓ Your upcoming open house

- ✓ Market statistics

- ✓ Mortgage rates

- ✓ A stunning new listing, viewed on property tour

What other situations with a built-in problem that needs solving, or unique benefits that need sharing, would make an interesting story answer? Choose one or three from the list above or make up you own and perfect practice your new answers to the question *"How's the real estate market?"* Give it a whirl; only good things can happen.

Getting Real – If It Was Easy, Everyone Would Do It

Psychologists tell us that creating new habits takes twenty-one repetitions. Be prepared to feel awkward and uncomfortable when you begin to replace your comfortable and formerly forgettable answers with new and engaging opportunity generators. Uncomfortable feelings are the natural consequences of shoving yourself beyond the fringes of your old comfort zone. Embrace and conquer this discomfort by doing what admired storytellers do: put your stories in writing, perfect practice your delivery, then share it—over and over.

Good luck, grace, and speed. Rise up.

I'm going to switch gears now. I'm going to move from natural laws and principles, psychology and psychographics, trust-building behaviors, mind and skill sets, to strategy and tactics, activities, and actions. Are you with me?

Okay, then. One for the money, two for the show, three to get ready and four to go, girl, go...

Chapter Thirteen

Is Misdirection Stunting Your Success?

"Learning is always rebellion... Every bit of new truth discovered is revolutionary to what was believed before."

~ Margaret Lee Runbeck, Author

You're not alone if you're feeling simultaneously swamped, successful, and stuck.

For Example . . .

I was chatting with Deborah. She's busy, busy, busy. Deborah has one teenage daughter, Lauren, and twins Heather and Nick, who are in the first grade; a chocolate Lab named Theo; a needy older sister; a conservative and white-collar husband; five salable listings; four sales in escrow; and a track record of Top Performance. Sounds like all systems are go, but it's not so. She feels her work-wheels are spinning. No matter how hard she works, she can't break through to a higher level of success – she's stuck. Deborah knows she needs to do something different, but she's not sure what. She feels she's doing the right things, but is sad that she doesn't have time to spend with her family. Working longer hours is definitely out.

We sat down and chatted about what was causing her to feel anxious, what she was doing, who she was doing it with, and how she was doing it. We were looking for clues as to what was stunting her efforts to create breakthrough success. We wanted to identify what could be tweaked and streamlined, the goal being to re-leverage her efforts, redirect off-target actions and activities, free up some time for the family, and jump her production to a new and higher level in the bargain.

As part of the process, we discussed which actions and activities were giving Deborah the *feeling* that she was being productive, then we compared them to the actions and activities that *truly and actually* generated business.

We discovered that the *true and actual* source for most of her business (around 70%) originated from people she knew personally, referral recommendations from her friends, past clients, and connections within her social networks. The rest of Deborah's business came from strangers responding to her advertising and marketing efforts: things like direct mail, print ads, open house, Internet leads, sign calls, and such.

Next we figured out where and on what she was spending her energy, time and money. Turns out she was spending about 75% of her finite resources chasing what generated only 25% of her business. She spent more time and money chasing and trying to attract strangers than she did engaging and connecting with people who already knew her, liked her and trusted her. This misdirection of resources was responsible for Deborah's stress, lack of family time, and stunted success.

Like Sherlock Holmes, we ultimately deduced that while Deborah was doing plenty right (Yay Deborah!), she was doing a handful of wrong things with the wrong people. We went on to talk about how, with a few swift tweaks, she could streamline her efforts by redirecting her actions and activities. This redirection would help Deborah recapture some precious time, and jump her business to a new level.

Here are some things we discovered that were stunting Deborah's business, and our streamlined solutions. See if you share any of them in common.

Stunting Belief: If you work hard, you'll be successful.

Streamlined Solution: Hard work alone does not Cruise Ship your career to success and fame. If you work hard but don't know where you want to end up, metaphorically, it's like working hard to straighten the deck chairs on the Lido Deck of the Titanic. Yeah, you're busy, but you're gonna sink.

For smooth sailing you want to chart your course with a simple written business plan.

Here's a simple plan for writing a simple business plan. Don't overcomplicate it; do write it down.

1. The first step is to think about what you want to accomplish. This is not about what others expect from you or want for you; it has to be what *you* want.

2. The second step, and I know you've heart it at least a hundred times before, put your specific plan in writing. Because you're reading this book, I know you're serious about your future; please don't skip this step. Get a blank sheet of paper and write it down now.

3. Next, break your plan down into specific and measurable mini-achievable parts. For example if your goal was production based you might write, "Take three new listings per month for a total of $500,000 in dollar volume. Make two sales per month for a total of $500,000 in volume. Close two sales per month for a total of$500,000 in volume.

4. Next, break your mini-achievable parts into micro-achievable actions. Using the example above, break your listing, sales, and closing goals down into daily activities and specific actions. I've included a Daily Activities Checklist at the end of this chapter. If you'd like a letter-sized .PDF version, send me an e-mail with DAC in the subject line and I'll hit you right back with a printable version. If you want to share a comment, that'd be super cool too. Here's the e-mail address: Ken@KenBrand.com. Or you're welcome to copy the worksheet from the book. Make ninety copies and use one every day for ninety days. Your awareness of where you're squandering your time will sharpen and your success will explode.

5. Lastly, work your plan like you're in it to win it.

See, this is simple. Like I said, don't complicate things – make your plan short and sweet, use one sheet of paper. Review your plan every morning and use the Daily Activities checklist every day for ninety days And whatever you do, don't spend all day on this exercise.

Stunting Activity: When my listings sell, I don't place a Sale Pending or Sold sign rider until I know the deal is solid, or shortly before closing.

Streamlined Solution: Sold listings are remarkable. Put your Sale Pending or Sold sign rider up immediately upon contract execution. Neighbors thinking of selling are attracted to SOLD listings and their listing agents. Neighbors are bored and embarrassed by unsold listings and unimpressed with their listing agents. Highlight your success, hit your high beams, and attract new opportunities!

Stunting Activity: Direct mail to my sphere doesn't seem to work and it kills trees, so I cut back to once a quarter, or whenever I have time and remember to do it.

Streamlined Solution: Savvy agent competitors are hustling to seduce and impress your current and future clients and friends. Sending a monthly, personalized and interesting direct mail piece, plus an evocative monthly e-mail or e-newsletter, is an important component of a well-rounded, Top of Mind Awareness marketing campaign*.

I know. Don't SPAM. After sending whatever you send, follow up with a personal contact to confirm they got it and ask if it's okay to continue. Following up to secure permission shows respect and courtesy.

*Note: If your direct mail campaign doesn't include In-Person contact and conversations with them, don't do it. Without personal contact it won't work, it's never worked, and it never will.

Stunting Activity: I'm on Facebook, but mostly I just look and lurk. I don't think I have anything interesting to say or post, so I usually don't.

Streamlined Solution: *A sense of significance* is a powerful human need. Interacting socially soothes and satisfies this human need and Facebook provides umpteen ways to acknowledge, engage, and share information with others. Daily engagement and contribution are key.

Status update daily! Don't stress over what clever things to say or share. You'll find that some of the popular, appreciated, and most-commented-on things are not clever, or pithy, they're simple things that people relate to. It's also considered good form, and generous, to share interesting things your friends post. With all your friends: share, share, share.

Oh, and it's okay and appreciated to click the LIKE button on other people's status updates and comments. Clicking the "LIKE" link is like smiling online. Do it often. You have a beautiful smile, share it with everyone.

Stunting Belief: I have a greenhouse of budding suspects and prospects, but because they aren't foaming at the mouth to buy or sell anytime soon, I put them on the back burner and rarely contact them. They love me; I know they'll call when they're ready.

Streamlined Solution: Personal circumstances can change in the blink of an eye. Yesterday's curious suspects can become today's hot opportunity. Stay in routine contact. If their situation turns unexpectedly from red to green, you'll be in position to know about it and help immediately.

Plus, if you set the table correctly and demonstrate trustworthiness, you can request and receive referral recommendations. Even if these folks never move, by nurturing trustworthy relationships and **Top of Mind Awareness**, you'll earn referral listings and boundless selling opportunities. Plus, staying in consistent contact with these people is an excellent **Three-People Principle** Opportunity.

Stunting Belief: I make lots of in-person contact, but because I just talked to them, I don't follow by mailing a handwritten note card. It seems redundant.

Streamlined Solution: Let me ask you, when was the last time you received a handwritten note in the mail? When it happened, how'd you feel about the person who took the time to write and send it to you? Exactly. If you want to stand out, make people feel good and be remembered, always follow up in-person conversations by mailing them a handwritten note. Remember to include two of your business cards.

P.S. This is a classic **Top of Mind Awareness** activity (Relevant, Remarkable, Repetition).

Stunting Belief: I know I have to make time to prospect for new business, but the day fills up with other important stuff and I have to be ready to help someone on a moment's notice. I have to stay flexible, fluid, and on call.

Streamlined Solution: Yes, you do have to stay flexible and fluid and no, you don't have to be on call. Yes, staying flexible and fluid is important, bend don't break, etc., but *on call*, NO. I see agents waiting all the time and getting ready to get ready. They look real busy, they feel busy, but nothing important is getting done. They are active but not productive.

You know how if you want to lose weight, all the Biggest Loser gurus will tell you that one of the keys to success is to track and record in writing everything you eat, how many calories everything you eat has in it, and when and where you ate what you ate? Personal accountability and awareness are important parts of going from too wide for your height, to just right. The same principle applies to your real estate business.

Get yourself a Moleskin or printed calendar type daybook and record in writing what you do all day. Write down the task you are doing, the time you started and ended – and, off to the side, how long it took you. Do this for one week without fail. I know, it's a pain in the butt, but I know that you know that one of the secrets to success is doing what others won't – starting tomorrow, *do this.*

What you're going to find out with this activity is how much of your valuable time you waste. Once you figure how much and what you waste your time on, you can streamline your day by time-blocking.

Time-blocking means that you simply and strictly schedule chunks of times to complete the important tasks of the day. When you've completed your important actions and activities for the day, you're done. Don't hang out and pussy-foot around with wasteful stuff or negative people. Instead, spend your recaptured time and energy on your personal stuff, like family, health, rest, renewal, fun, and relaxation.

Stunted Belief: I don't have time to work out, play with the kids, GNO (Girls Night Out), make love, pamper myself, or take wild adventure vacations or an occasional nap.

Streamlined Belief: Yes, you do. But a busy and dedicated person like yourself will never *find* the time to put yourself before others, you have to *make* the time by time-blocking your personal time like you do for listing and showing appointments. You'd never cancel an important appointment with a client unless it was a real emergency, would you? You should treat yourself and the people you love at least as importantly as your clients.

To handle your responsibilities while you're unavailable (personal time), choose a trustworthy working partner. When you take time off, bring your working partner completely up to speed on what might show up in your absence. Trust, release, and enjoy your time off; it's essential to a healthy mind, body, soul, business, and your love life.

Stunted Activity: I'm spending cash and credit on newspaper, magazine, and traditional forms of advertising because sellers like it. I see other top producers doing it too, so it must be the right thing to do. Plus, I've always done it, so I'm afraid to stop.

Streamlined Activity: Analyze the true source of your business for the past six months. Define where your business truly and actually came from. Also analyze and document where and how much you're spending on advertising, marketing, and personal promotion.

Most agents discover that they're spending the majority of their marketing money on things that generate the least amount of business, just as Deborah was doing. If that's the case with you too, redirect your marketing dollars. Invest your resources in building relationships and creating **Top of Mind Awareness** with the people who like you, trust you, choose you, refer you, and recommend you.

At least four times a year, sit quietly, gather your thoughts and repeat this exercise. What's paying for itself and what's not? Consider which activities and behaviors work for you, and which work against you. Then make your thoughtful adjustments. Do this and you'll jump your success to new levels.

Hip-Hip-Hoorah!

We've reached the point where we better understand our business and more deeply understand ourselves and what's been holding us back from the true success we deserve. Now it's time to play with some fun strategies. In the next section you'll find over forty proven and simple to do "How-tos" that you can put into play *today* to stratosphere your success.

P.S. Here's that daily checklist I told you about. Make ninety copies and use one every day. Please.

It Takes Contact To Make Contracts
Daily Checklist / Date_____

Personal Sphere: Total #:_____ #Added_____

Of In-Person Contacts:_____

Of Phone Contacts:_____

of Note Cards Sent:____ _____

Of Direct Mail Pieces Sent:_____

of eCards Sent:_____

# of eNewsletters Sent:_____

# of Note Cards Sent:_____

Facebook Friends: Total #:_____ #Added_____

Of Status Updates____ _____

Of Links Shared_____

Of "Likes" Clicked____ _____

Of Video/Photos Shares_____

Of Comments Made_____

"How's The Real Estate Market" Questions Answered?

Of Stories Shared:_____

Of Business Cards Shared:_____

Of Referrals Asked For:_____

OPEN HOUSE

Of Invitations Mailed:_____

Of In-Person Invitations Made:_____

Of Phone Invitations Made:____ _____

Of Prospects Met:___ # Of Note Cards Sent:____

Prospect Follow Up Contacts Made:_____

Of Appointments Set:_____

Of Note Cards Sent:_____

eMail Auto-Notification Enrolment

Of New Enrollments:_____

Of Notifications Received Today:_____

Of Phone Conversations:_____

Of In-Person Conversations:_____

Of Note Cards Sent:_____

Geographic Neighborhood Farming: Total #____

Of In-Person Contacts:_____

Of Phone Contacts:____ _____

of Note Cards Sent:_____

Of Direct Mail Pieces Sent:_____ _____

of eCards Sent: #_____

# of eNewsletters Sent:_____

# of Note Cards Sent:_____

Just Sold/Listed Quantum Mail Post Cards

Mailed:____ # Of Phone Contacts:_____

Of In-Person Contacts:_____

Of Note Cards Sent:_____

Listing Presentations Made:_____

Buyer Clients Shown:_____

Contracts Written (Seller or Buyer):_____

STAGE III:

"Without strategy, execution is aimless. Without execution, strategy is useless."

- Morris Chang

Chapter Fourteen

How to Gossip Your Way to the Closing Table

"Gossip is just news running ahead of itself in a red satin dress."

– Liz Smith

Want to look whip-smart, spark conversation, boost your **Top of Mind Awareness** and create a sweet flowing stream of commission checks via referrals from your friends? Without annoying them? Please say *yes,* because then I can share how weaving good gossip can accomplish just that.

Now we know that most gossip is mean-spirited, a breach of trust and the kiss of death for a real estate agent. I want you to avoid mean gossip at all costs. What I'm talking about in this chapter is good gossip: the kind of gossip that is positive, friendly, and appreciated.

What I want you to do is share good gossip with your cheerleader friends. But before I tell you how and why, let me ask you this. How many cheerleader friends do you have?. Cheerleader friends are your true and beautiful friends who root for you unconditionally, are eager to support and help you, and are always happy to hear from you. So how many of those do you have? Seven, nineteen, or fifty-seven? Do you have your number in mind? Great. With your cheerleader friends in mind, let's look at how we can strategically share good gossip and enrich our friends and ourselves in the process.

Our good gossip strategy begins with a look at human behavior.

Let's Explore Human Nature

Let me ask you four questions about human nature in general:

1. When a fresh "For Sale" sign sprouts up in a neighborhood, do the neighbors wonder what the list price is?

2. When a neighborhood listing goes under contract and the listing agent slaps up a red SOLD sign rider, would that event be viewed as interesting news by the neighbors?

3. When a property in their neighborhood is "sold" and "closed," are the neighbors cat-curious about how much the property sold for?

4. Do people enjoy juicy gossip? Gossip, like pictures of what the inside of their neighbor's house looks like, listing prices, price reductions, and sold information ?

When I ask these questions in a classroom setting, most everyone agrees, curiosity about real estate activity in his or her neighborhood is a natural human behavior. This is proven out because if you're using Take One Flyers on your listings, why do you think they all disappear and you get zero phone calls for more information? It's because the neighbors snuck down and grabbed a flyer. Most of the neighbors want to know what their neighbors are up to, including all the juicy real estate-related details. Agreed?

Now let me ask you three questions about yourself, then I'll share what and how to take advantage of human behavior and enrich you and your friends in the process. The three questions are:

1. Would you like to be THE good gossip news provider for real estate activity in your cheerleader friends' neighborhoods?

2. Would providing your cheerleader friends with real-time neighborhood market news make you appear even more majestically savvy, plugged in, and supremely worthy of referrals?

3. Would you enjoy a positive and comfortable reason to engage in appreciated chit-chat (aka good gossip) with a true friend, a friend who delights in referring you business?

More on Good Gossip Strategy, Cheerleaders, and Commission Checks

About now you may be thinking, "*My cheerleader friends may never move, what's the point?*" No worries, this isn't about your friends moving, it's about these three things:

Three Things That Matter:

1. **The Three-People Principle**: Everyone, including your cheerleader friends, knows three people that move in a year.

2. Your cheerleader friends are curious about real estate activity in their neighborhood, as everyone else is. Providing real-time, in their neighborhood, real estate updates (good gossip), enhances your professional image, strengthens **Top of Mind Awareness,** and creates an opportunity for in-person and on-purpose conversations.

3. Conversations with friends deepen relationships and provide a relaxed and natural opportunity for your cheerleader friends to share referrals and recommendations.

With these three things in mind to keep your cheerleaders informed and in the know, all you need is a simple three-step strategy to get your good gossip campaign started.

And Here It Is:

Step 1. Identify your cheerleader friends. Confirm you have their phone numbers, e-mails, and mailing addresses. (I know, "duh," work with me here.) If you don't have this contact information, get it.

Step 2. Using your Multiple Listing Service (MLS) system, or whatever system works for you, set-up an e-mail auto-notification/alert for any real estate activity on their street and immediate neighborhood. Yes, that's right; all activity, by which I mean new listings, price changes, pending sales, closed sales, expired listings, terminated listings, and price changes. Do not have your auto-notification/alert program send the e-mail directly to your friends. Have the auto e-mail notification/alert sent directly to you.

Step 3. When you receive an auto-notification/alert, pick up the phone, call your cheerleader friend and share the information. After you hang up, write a quick note, include two business cards, drop your note card in the mail, and then forward the email alert to your friend.

Pretty simple, eh? If you're already doing something like this, rock ON. If you're not gossiping your way to the closing table, get to it and let me know how it goes. [Ken@KenBrand.com]

Remember the idea here is to keep your friends informed, demonstrate that you have your thumb on the pulse of the market, strengthen your **Top of Mind Awareness**, and position yourself to receive referrals via **The Three-People Principle**.

Oh, and by the way, it's a fine idea to set auto-notifications/alerts for all your active listings as well. The last thing you want is for your seller to call and ask you about the new listing down the street, and you don't have clue one what they're talking about!

One last thing, I've included this activity It Takes Contact to Make Contracts Daily Worksheet I shared at the end of Chapter Thirteen.

It Takes Contact To Make Contracts
Daily Checklist / Date_____

Personal Sphere: Total #:_____ #Added_____

Of In-Person Contacts:_____

Of Phone Contacts:_____

of Note Cards Sent:____ _____

Of Direct Mail Pieces Sent:_____

of eCards Sent:_____

# of eNewsletters Sent:_____

# of Note Cards Sent:_____

Facebook Friends: Total #:_____ #Added_____

Of Status Updates____ _____

Of Links Shared_____

Of "Likes" Clicked____ _____

Of Video/Photos Shares_____

Of Comments Made_____

"How's The Real Estate Market" Questions Answered?

Of Stories Shared:_____

Of Business Cards Shared:_____

Of Referrals Asked For:_____

OPEN HOUSE

Of Invitations Mailed:_____

Of In-Person Invitations Made:_____

Of Phone Invitations Made:_____

Of Prospects Met:____ # Of Note Cards Sent:____

Prospect Follow Up Contacts Made:_____

Of Appointments Set:_____

Of Note Cards Sent:_____

eMail Auto-Notification Enrolment

Of New Enrollments:_____

Of Notifications Received Today:_____

Of Phone Conversations:_____

Of In-Person Conversations:_____

Of Note Cards Sent:_____

Geographic Neighborhood Farming: Total #____

Of In-Person Contacts:_____

Of Phone Contacts:____ _____

of Note Cards Sent:_____

Of Direct Mail Pieces Sent:____ _____

of eCards Sent: #_____

# of eNewsletters Sent:_____

# of Note Cards Sent:_____

Just Sold/Listed Quantum Mail Post Cards

Mailed:____ # Of Phone Contacts:_____

Of In-Person Contacts:_____

Of Note Cards Sent:_____

Listing Presentations Made:_____

Buyer Clients Shown:_____

Contracts Written (Seller or Buyer):_____

Chapter Fifteen

How to Navigate the Social Media and Cyber Space Frontiers.

"The future has already happened. It's just not evenly distributed."

- Adrian Slywotzky, Mercer Consultants

Facebook and Google are like the Pacific and Atlantic oceans. Only instead of oceans of water, they're oceans of information.

Google fills its ocean with indexed and catalogued web pages, blog posts, online advertising, status updates, uploaded pictures, videos, and on and on. If it happens online, it flows into the Google Ocean and stays there forever and ever and ever.

Facebook fills its ocean with the social things that its 600 million-and-growing users do on Facebook. Personal things like: *"I'm-doing-this-now"* status updates, *"Here's pictures and videos of me, my family and friends"*, *"I 'Like, this,"* *"I have a 'comment' about that,"* and on and on.

Both oceans of information are growing at a wild pace. The depth and breadth of information is staggering, and is matched by the numbers of people and the frequency with which they turn to one or both of the information oceans for answers, solutions, character confirmation, socializing, and entertainment. Forrester Research, an internationally recognized technology consulting firm, released a study December of 2010 that stated, *"For the first time ever, the average US online consumer spends as much time online as he or she does watching TV offline."* What do you imagine this means to you and me and our other real estate friends?

I think it means two things. First, learning how to use the Internet, Facebook, Google, and other online services to help us succeed and best serve our clients isn't an a wouldn't-it-be-nice option any more. It's a Must Do. There are plenty of books on how to walk on social media water and master the power of the Internet. I recommend two, both were written by Chris Brogan; *Social Media 101,* published by John Wiley & Sons, Inc., 2009, and

Trust Agents, also published by John Wiley & Sons Inc., 2010. I recommend you read them both right after you finish this one.

Secondly, as hundreds of millions turn more frequently to the Internet as the resource and authority for real estate information, including character-confirmation and answers to their big and small questions, the importance of our being easily found cannot be overemphasized. Being found on the Internet is the focus of this chapter.

Here's an Example of Why This Is Important

Ken and Robyn decide to sell their house and buy a better one. They know half a dozen real estate agents from the hundreds in the community to choose from. They put their heads together and narrow their choice of agents down to two. Ken and Robyn are keenly interested in things like marketing examples, peer recommendations, web savvy, character, market knowledge, reputation, experience, and trustworthiness, so they turn to Google and Facebook to conduct their research.

Each agent's name is typed into the search box and, instantly, all the individual bits and pages of information are served up. Ken and Robyn discover that Betty has only two links of information and those were served up on page four. Also, it looks like Betty might be on Facebook, but they can't be sure if the Betty they found is the Betty they are looking for. There's no profile picture, no contact information, and no activity.

They decide to forget about Betty and type Darlene's name into the search box. Darlene is even more invisible than Betty. Ken and Robyn cross Betty and Darlene off their list.

Time for Plan B

They choose another two agents recommended by a trusted friend and search again. This time, Michelle and Katie both dominate the first page in their Google search. Clicking around, Robyn and Ken confirm that both of their choices are active, engaged, and knowledgeable. Their online behavior and published material suggest they are also trustworthy and experienced.

Ken and Robyn set appointments to interview Michelle and Katie.

Isn't that what you do when you want to check something or someone out? Of course. We all do. And that trend is growing faster than the average and ordinary agent is responding to it. Which is an advantage for you.

If you're not quickly findable via a Google Search, and if your Facebook presence is puny, or you're still making *"I'm technology challenged"* excuses and apologies, then I have wicked bad news. You're becoming an invisible and irrelevant agent. If you don't dive in head first, soon you'll be out of the business, just like Darlene and Betty.

Diving in

Whether you're just now dipping your toes in, full-blown swimming, or you're standing on the shore ready to splash in, what you learn in this chapter will help you succeed in the Internet era. Also, I encourage you to read those two books I recommended earlier. If you have an iPad or a Kindle, you can download them instantly. That's the new world we live in.

To make sure that who and what we are (character confirmation, peer recommendations, agent ratings), and that what we do can do for others (samples, examples, and resources) can be found online, we have to create our own body of information water. The more content and personal information we upload, share, and post online, the more findable we become. Here's more detail on how it works.

For you, me, and our competitors, each of our online engagements is like a tiny personalized water drop of information. Things like status updates, comments, check-ins, and every single bit of online stuff published by us, such as blog posts, web pages, uploaded videos (Youtube.com), pictures (Facebook.com & Flickr.com), presentations (SlideShare.com & Scribd.com) and online advertising campaigns. All our online information water drops, whether by personal engagement or personal publishing, are cataloged, indexed, and ranked by Google and Facebook and added to the endlessly deep Google and Facebook oceans. The more catalogued and indexed drops of information we have, the more discoverable we become.

Becoming Discoverable Online

There are many places, ways, and means to take advantage of online publishing and engagement. But since I'm assuming you don't have infinite time or super-thick patience, I'd recommend the following five most significant opportunities:

> ➢ Facebook.com: Facebook is omnipresent and THE MOST important conversation, connection, trust-building, and personal broadcasting tool on planet Earth. The more you engage, share, and broadcast on Facebook,

the easier it is to find and learn more about you. (Unless your security settings nix it. I wouldn't nix it.)

Here's a sample of what some of my Facebook real estate agents had to share about the matter on my page.

Ken Brand

🏢 Sales Manager at Prudential Gary Greene, Realtors - The Woodlands TX / 832-797-1779 🎓 Studied Life Long Learning, Leaderhsip, Persuasion, Communicaiton Arts at Blood, Sweat, Sandpaper & Tears 🏠 Lives in The Woodlands, Texas 💗 Married to Robyn Brand 🏠 From San Diego, California 🎂 Born on October 26 ✏ Edit Profile

Share: 🖳 Status 📷 Photo ⚲ Link ◻ Video

 Wall
🔲 Info
📷 Photos (137)
🗨 Questions
📄 Notes
👥 Friends

Married to

Robyn Brand

Friends (4702)

 Ken Brand
Dear Real Estate Friends - I'm almost done with my book project and I was wondering if you could do me a favor. In the social media chapter of my book (Less Blah-Blah, More Ah-Ha - A modern guide to social selling and sweet success) i'd like to include your social media success story. If you've had some cool or profitable success (listings/sales/referrals) by using Facebook, Twitter, Your Blog, LinkedIn (social media stuff) if you'll leave your short and sweet story in the comments, my aim is to include them in the book. See the vid for more details. So, can you help a brother out? Thanks man. Cheers.

 Ken needs more help than usual. . . [HQ]
Length: 2:26

◻ Friday at 2:45pm · Like · Comment · Share

👍 Gina Kay Landis and Becky Boomsma like this.

 Matt Thomson Last summer I sold a waterfront home to some cash buyers from Taiwan. They were moving to Gig Harbor, WA, from Taiwan, and as an avid photographer the husband had Googled "Wildlife photos of Gig Harbor." My blog came up #2 on page 1 with a photo of a bald eagle eating a salmon that I had posted. He "lurked" on my blog for 5 months prior to contacting me, then introduced himself on my blog comments. Less than 70 days later, they were in the States and in their new home in Gig Harbor!
Friday at 4:33pm · Unlike · 👍 4 people

Debra Kinkaid Kipple I had kept in touch on a sporadic and infrequent basis with a friend from 7th grade whom I hadn't seen since then (1972). I found her on Facebook last year and when her father died, got the listing. Had I not advertised being a Realtor on Facebook, i do not believe that she would have chosen me.

Same situation with a schoolmate from my high school German class. We hadn't communicated since then, but upon becoming Facebook friends last year, she solicited my services when she needed a home to rent recently upon her move from California to The Woodlands.
Friday at 5:22pm · Unlike · 👍 1 person

 Jim Canion This is good news Ken. Cant wait to see more of your own original style of off the wall, Wizard Academy slant on life and real estate. Facebook
is best way to open up to the world for all to see who you are. Found a friend from high school r...
See More
Saturday at 5:49am · Unlike · 👍 1 person

 Ian Lazarus Ken, In 09 and 10 I closed 9 deals from FB alone. 8 incoming and 1 outgoing. Also helped 8-10 other FB friends put agents together.
Yesterday at 9:28am · Unlike · 👍 1 person

Here are five pointers to streamline your success on Facebook:

1. Completely and thoroughly flesh out your online profile, including your profile picture. This is important because the more information you share about yourself, the more others can get to know you. People trust people they know and distrust strangers.

2. As you meet new people in real life, friend them on Facebook.

3. Comment on others people's status updates; commenting is similar to In Real Life conversation, only it's happening in cyberspace. Click the "Like" link a lot – this is like smiling at someone IRL.

4. Wish people Happy Birthday.

5. Share pictures, videos, and web links to things you find interesting or helpful. This helps you show your personality, interests, and hobbies. Remember the 80% personal and 20% business rules of sharing and engagement.

6. Shoot for at least thirty minutes of Facebook time per day; it's not a toy or a fad, it's a free tool.

Make friends with Facebook and you'll become omnipresent within your networks and niches.

> Blog: A blog is an excellent way to share relevant information, hyper-local real estate information, and content that show-cases your expertise. A blog also pro-vides you with a platform to demonstrate your trustworthiness. Getting started is easier than ever – check with your local REALTOR Association for classes and recommendations.

> SlideShare.com: All those presentations, marketing materials, flyers, brochures, and printables – all that valuable stuff you've squirreled away in a dented file cabinet – can now be stored digitally and shared online in your personal and free SlideShare.com account. SlideShare.com makes shar-ing your stuff easily discoverable and share-able. Also, because your good stuff is now online and digital, it has a unique online web-link address – this means you can quickly and easily share it on Facebook, in your emails and anywhere you can include a web link. Get rid of those dented file cabi-nets and mountains of paper; store your stuff in a cloud like SlideShare.com

> YouTube.com: Think about the conse-quences and repercussions of this: Google, which owns YouTube, now uses speech

recognition to index and catalogue each and every uploaded video. This is huge! It means that anything you talk about in your videos can show up in a relevant Google search. For example, if you upload a video of your most recent raving fan sharing their story about how awesome you are, it may show up when someone Googles your name.

Creating and uploading small video clips about commonly asked real estate questions (topics including: property appraisals, current market statistics, neighborhood overviews, client testimonials, etc.) would be wise. Plus, like most everything uploaded to the Internet cloud, web links to your uploaded videos can be shared via places like Facebook and e-mail.

If you haven't created your personal YouTube.com account, do it today, http://www.youtube.com/create_account

> Smart Phone: Your smart phone allows for fast and simple online sharing (posting), and conversation—all in the palm of your hand. There's an app for anything you can think of. So find the useful ones and use them. While you're out and about working, playing, loving, and living, upload and share photos and short videos, post status updates, share observations, check in and

broadcast to your Facebook, Flickr, and Youtube accounts. Using your smart phone, it's easier than ever to share, contribute, and engage. Train yourself to do it daily.

Yeah, I know. All of this online whiz-bang and social media hoopla can feel foreign and look suspiciously like a time-suck vortex. It's not! Get that thought out of your head; devil be gone.

The Internet represents the biggest opportunity in the real estate business since the cell phone. Starting today, open your mind, stretch your imagination, and become friends with the Web in general and social media specifically.

The best time to get started is now. If you want to see examples of what I'm talking about, take a look at these websites.

www.Facebook.com/KenBrand

www.SlideShare.com/KenBrand

www.Flickr.com/Kens411

www.LinkedIn.com/KenBrand

www.Twitter.com/KenBrand

www.BrandCandid.com

Chapter Sixteen

How to Turn Your Messages
from Lightning Bugs to Lightning Bolts

"Clarity is more important than creativity."

*~ Roy H. Williams, Global Advertising Consultant,
Wizard of Ads*

If you want to pogo to the pro level and move from Blah-Blah to Ah-Ha, you'll want to focus your marketing, presentations, and conversations with the clarifying lens of context.

**Context sharpens clarity.
Clarity creates relevance and Ah-Ha
understanding.
Understanding creates trust.
Trust attracts.**

Attraction leads to being chosen and referral recommendations.

Context Sharpens Clarity

Minus context, our messages are received as fuzzy, out of focus, and either uncertain or untrue bullshit. Avoid the fuzzy whenever possible, by adding context and detail.

Clarity Creates Ah-Ha Understanding

Adding a layer of context and detail to what we're sharing is the tiny extra effort that moves what we have to say and share from featherweight and fuzzy to clear and understood

Understanding Creates Trust

Consumers are naturally suspicious and skeptical. Because they're bombarded with thousands of buy-this, buy-me, and trust-me marketing messages a day, they keep their BS detector in always-on mode, and their guard up. Generally people ignore the common and predictable sales pitch, shun the unsafe, and distrust the unfamiliar and uncertain.

Adding context and detail to our marketing messages and conversations makes the relevance and the benefits of what we're sharing under-stood. When others understand where we're coming from and how what we're sharing clearly benefits *them*, not us, they are more likely to trust us.

Trust Attracts

We're all attracted to people and things we trust. Simple, huh? It's no more than connecting the dots.

Attraction Leads to Being Chosen and Referral Recommendations

If you behave in trustworthy ways, people will trust you. People are attracted to people they trust. People choose to buy things and hire people they trust. They also share, refer, and recommend trustworthy things and people to their friends, neighbors, coworkers, and relatives.

Let Me Add Some Context and Detail to How to Add Context and Detail

Adding context and detail is fairly simple. I say it's simple because you already know what you need to know. Like most of the things that will move you way past bumpkin-ordinary, all you need to do is connect the dots and put what you already know into action.

Let me share a few fuzzy, uncertain, and usually ignored message examples, along with a new and improved version that includes context and detail. As you'll see, the difference seems subtle, but the impact of how the message is received is the difference between a lightning bug and a lightning bolt.

Lightning Bug Statement: Mortgage rates are at an all-time low – buy now.

Lightning Bolt Statement: Mortgage rates are at an all time low of 5%. That means for every $1,000 dollars borrowed, the monthly payment on a thirty-year mortgage is only $5.37 per month. A $300,000 mortgage would be only $1,611 per month.

Lightning Bug Statement: We sell homes for top dollar.

Lightning Bolt Statement: We sell homes for top dollar! According to Multiple Listing Service Statistics, the average sold price to list price percentage for homes in our market area is 94.5%. Our office average is a full 2% higher. It's 96.7%. What that means is, with an average sold price in our market of $350,000, we net our sellers an additional $7,000 compared to the average.

Lightning Bug: We sell homes fast.

Lightning Bolt: We sell homes fast. According to the Multiple Listing Service Statistics, the average number of days on market (DOM) for sold homes in our market area is 110 days. Our office average is 77 DOM.

There you have it. Listen, you're already saying and sharing things. With a little awareness and re-tweaking, you can easily add context and detail to your everyday conversations. Here's a small four-stepper to get you rolling.

Try This Four-Step Lightning Bolt Action Plan:

1. Evaluate your written and spoken marketing messages. Include your listing presentation, marketing materials, how you answer questions, and your online and offline advertising and promotional materials.

2. Look for and delete the loosely defined and fuzzily described.

3. Add context and detail where necessary.

4. Re-launch, re-engage, and reap the rewards of contextual clarity.

Chapter Seventeen

How to Go from Zero in Escrow to Boo-Yah in Thirty Days or Less

"You sort of start thinking anything's possible if you've got enough nerve."

~ J. K. Rowling

Big problem. You're sipping tall, iced Cinnamon Dolce Lattes. Chit-chatting. Your girlfriend Sally shares, "I need to make a sale in the next thirty-seven days or I have to quit the business." She confesses, "I don't have a single active listing, or any qualified buyers."

She's broke in bank and spirit. She's frowning, drowning, and three quarters dead in the water. She pleads for your advice, "*What should I do? I need to make a sale NOW!*"

What advice would you share?

What do you believe is the most productive thing Sally can do to position herself to make the required sale and resuscitate her long-term success? If she doesn't make a sale in the next thirty-seven days, she's cooked.

Here's What I'd Do . . .

First, I'd give her a big hug. Then I'd tell her that she can make it happen if she wants to, but it won't be easy. Given that there's not enough time to focus on taking a listing, odds are it would take too long to sell. So, a laser focus on attracting a qualified buyer is what's required.

Next, I'd advise her to use "The Jesse James Solution." Yep, it's time to get her Jesse James ON! Whoa! Not Sandra Bullock's wayward Jesse James, this one:

Judge Roy Bean: "*Why do you rob banks?*"

Jesse James: "*Because that's where the money is.*"

I'd implore my friend Sally to hold public open houses. Ten public open houses in thirty days.

Why? Because like Jesse James knew where the money was, in the real estate biz holding an open house event is where she'll find buyers.

Even in this whiz-bang Internet era of ubiquitous online property listing information, buyers still browse open houses, sometimes in droves.

Holding an open house event is an activity that allows Sally an opportunity to take swift and strong action, make contact, and weave renewed success. You know, instead of hoping and waiting.

I'll explain where, when, and how to get the best results, in open house event tips below. But first, let's understand what an open house event is **not**. It's **not** showing up late, planting a couple of directionals, flipping the lights on, lighting a prayer candle, and hoping something lucky happens. It rarely does. Lady Luck mostly ignores the lazy and befriends the bold. Read on to find out what an open house event **IS**.

Back to our broken friend Sally. Like I said, I'd tell her to hold ten open house events in thirty days. Strategically selected, well-planned, powerfully promoted, and passionately executed. Here are the tips I mentioned earlier.

Open House Event Tips

When: Now! Today! The sooner the better. Hold open house events on late afternoons and early evening weekdays. Open house signs spied on weekdays and on the way home from work are unusual, and therefore attract attention, which generates traffic.

Hold open house events Saturday and Sunday afternoons (2 p.m. to 5 p.m.). Your mission, should you accept it: hold Ten Open House Events in thirty days. You have permission to do more.

Where: Pick a property that is supremely attractive, easy to find with directional arrows ,and is priced in the sweet spot (what's selling) for your market area. You can research what's selling best by consulting your Multiple Listing Service. Ideally, you will want to pick a property that was recently listed, the fewer days on market the better. If you don't have a listing that qualifies, no worries, don't let that sink or slow you. Ask your teammates if you can hold one or more of their listings open. Most importantly, don't pick any random property. Choose strategically. Umm-hmm.

The How-tos (thirteen of them!):

1. Promote your open house online at Trulia. com, Zillow.com, Realtor.com, your blog,

Facebook Business Page, Twitter, Association, and brokerage websites.

2. Make seventy-one color open house flyer announcements/invitations. Don't spend all day creating a flyer. Get this chore done fast. The magic is not in what the flyer looks like; the magic is you and what you do with the flyer.

3. Mail twenty-one of your open house flyers as invitations, to your current nest of buyers prospects/suspects and twenty-three to your most enthusiastic cheerleader friends.

4. Follow up your mailed invitation flyers with phone calls. Say "Hello,"ask if they received your flyer, and invite them to share your flyer invitation with anyone they think might be interested. The main thing is that this action provides you with the opportunity to have On-Purpose and In-Person conversations with people who like, trust, and would happily recommend you. Having conversations with your cheerleader friends, and current buyer prospects and suspects, unlocks possibilities and opportunities. Follow up each phone call with a hand-written, short-n-sweet note and drop it in the mail with two of your business cards.

5. Hand-deliver your open house flyer invitations to twenty-seven neighbors. Yes. I do mean personally knock on their door and invite them, ending your conversations with this question: *"When we sell this home, would you like to know how much it SOLD for?"* If they say yes, get their contact information, add them to your database, set up an automated activity notification (like we talked about for your cheerleader friends in Chapter Fourteen). Begin including them in your personal marketing and relationship building campaign, and keep them informed of all new real estate activity in their neighborhood. Remember to write a short-n-sweet note (nice to meet you and other pleasantries) and drop it in the mail with two of your business cards.

6. If you are planting an open house sign on the edge of someone's property, knock on their door, smile, politely ask for permission, and invite them to your open house. Remember to ask them if they'd like to know what your listing sells for. If they say "yes,"what should you do next? (Clue: re-read How-to #5.)

7. Do your homework about the neighborhood. Preview active listings in the neighborhood (in person, not online), research recent sales, and

familiarize yourself with the local schools, parks, grocery stores, and local knowledge.

8. Set the stage – lights, blinds, aroma, and music – no TV watching. When you're finished, make sure you put everything back where it belongs. Especially, check that the lights and the heating and cooling are reset to how you found them, and that doors and windows are locked.

9. During slow traffic periods, use your cell phone to make the touching-base phone calls you know you should be making, but haven't. Even if nobody shows up at your open house event, if you spend your time making In-Person and On-Purpose contacts, you're working hard and making good things happen. You can't go from broke to boo-yah without contact and conversations. Call. Contact. Call. Then call and contact some more.

10. At the conclusion of the open house, send thank you cards to everyone who attended.

11. If you held someone else's house open, report your results to the listing agent so they can report to their seller. This is professional, polite, and appreciated behavior.

12. Follow up, follow up, and follow up some more – with all prospects.

13. Hold an open house event at least ten times in the next thirty days.

Don't Overcomplicate or Overthink It – Do It

Listen, if like Sally, the end of your career is near if you don't sell something fast, or you simply want to create sexy success now, you need to take dramatically **bold** action and amp everything up. As if your career depends on it. Because it does.

The main thing is to get started right now: Make contact with your cheerleader friends, talk to the neighbors, send follow-up notecards, preview new properties, learn new neighborhoods, and meet new people who need help buying or selling. Every day is precious. Now is the time. Get started right now. If you do this with passion, positive things WILL happen, and instead of mourning the end of your real estate career, you'll be celebrating the beginning of your boo-yah renewal, reward, and redemption.

P.S. Where and when is your next open house event?

Chapter Eighteen

How to Adopt Abandoned Buyers

"I always wanted to be successful, not famous."

~ George Harrison, Beatle

Does Closing and Running = Abandonment?

Sadly for them, the majority of average and ordinary selling agents do not stay in touch with buyer clients after closing. They think that when the deal is done it's time to run. Fresh leads need chasing, and an uncertain future needs feeding.

At first blush, "closing and running" seems logical, maybe even smart. The rationale is (by those average and ordinary selling agents) that gleefully-settled buyers won't be moving for years, so why waste precious attention on a multi-years-distant possibility? Bills need to be paid now. Right?

Dead Wrong! Closing and running is abandonment and financially unwise. Here's why.

The magical power of **The Three-People Principle** is supreme. Okay, it's not really magical, but it is pretty supreme – and based in fact. Closed buyer clients who chose you and trusted you to represent them will, within the next year, know of three people who are going to make a move and need the services of a Wonder Woman real estate such as yourself. Invest time and attention in these fine folks and you'll earn referral recommendations. Referrals are the best leads, are they not? And they're free. Well, almost free. You have to invest some emotional labor to remain relevant and remarkable, and therefore referrable. But that's easy; it's what you do—or, what you will be doing once you've read and implemented the ideas in this book, right?

So, are we agreed that staying close and relevant is smart and profitable? Hope so.

But wait, there's even a higher, Sensi-like level of business cultivation. The wise capitalize by monetizing the mistakes of the average and ordinary majority. Some weaklings might consider this business-getting tactic "stealing." I call it smart and Adopting Abandoned Buyers.

Adopting Abandoned Buyers: The Strategy

This Zen strategy is pretty straightforward. Most selling agents abandon their buyers after closing. When you're the listing agent, grow your success by cultivating a relationship of relevancy and trust with the abandoned buyer of your listing. Yes. You heard right. I believe you should adopt the abandoned buyer, and become their Go-to-Girl for all things home, community, lifestyle, and real estate.

Let me share a four-step action plan that I've used and profited from.

1. After closing, mail a handwritten note card. Wish them well, welcome them to their new and wonderful home, the neighborhood, etc. Of course, include two of your business cards.

2. Thirteen days after closing, between 2:37 p.m. and 7:57 p.m., stop by their home, in person, to see how things are going. Ask for permission to stay in touch. I'd say something like this, "Hey, would it be okay if I touched base from time to time to see if I could be helpful with anything real estate related?" or "Hey,

I mail monthly real estate market report updates to my friends. I'd like to include you – would you be offended if I shared my real estate market report with you too?"

3. Follow up this visit by mailing a handwritten note card (nice talking to you, short-n-sweet). Use purple ink, a single sheet of canary yellow shaded paper, a hot-pink envelope and a real postage stamp, preferably one with an eagle or American flag on it. Ha ha, just kidding. Doesn't matter what time you stop by or what color combo stationery you choose. It only matters that you Do It.

4. Stay in touch. Remember the value of including these fine folks (the ones who gave you permission to stay in touch) in your thoughtfully created and wisely managed **Top of Mind Awareness** campaign (relevant, remarkable, repetitious contact, conversations, and engagement).

Pretty simple approach, but uncommon. You know what you need to do. Go for it. Er, not next week. Like, right now! Cool.

Chapter Nineteen

How Not to Flub Future Referrals and Recommendations.

"You are the only person on earth who can use your ability."

~ M. Kathleen Casey

It's why we do all the bone-crushing, attitude-straining, heartfelt work. We work to create and earn confidence and trust. When we succeed, people we know refer people they know to us. Sweet success, right?

Sort of.

What I mean is, it's epic to earn a referral recommendation, but we need to ensure that in our rush to help and deliver, we don't flub our future by forgetting to show appreciation to the people who refer us. If we handle our referral business smartly, behaving in ways that reinforce the free-flow of future referrals, we can turn a singular golden referral opportunity into a perpetually pro-ducing referral gold mine.

In a moment we're going to check out how to do just that. But first, let's take a look at how future referrals and recommendations are flubbed.

Riley Foster, a motivated and qualified civilian calls Lois Lane the real estate agent, referred by Robyn, a mutual and trusted friend. "Hi Lois, my name is Riley Foster. We don't know each other, but our mutual friend Robyn Brand referred me to you. She said you were a great real estate agent, and I should talk to you about selling my house and buying a new one."

Lois grips the phone tighter, goes giddy and does a happy dance. Woo-whoooo, sweet Jiminy Cricket. Life is grand, Lois takes a lay down listing and is set to sell Riley something new too. Amen.

Lois goes right to work, hyper-focused on doing a proud job. In all the excitement, Lois does not immediately call the friend who referred this golden opportunity. In fact, Lois is so busy, and focused on doing a great job, that she neglects to touch base with her referring friend Robyn—until after the closing.

The scenario I just shared doesn't sound bad – in fact it sounds normal, and a late thank you is better than no follow-up or thank you at all. But here's the problem. During the transaction, Lois doesn't keep her referring friend informed. By keeping silent, Lois keeps her deep appreciation and success a secret. When our cheerleader friends don't feel appreciated and acknowledged for referring us business, the likelihood of receiving future referrals is diminished.

Thankfully, these flubs can be fixed. Earning a free-flow of future qualified referrals is fun, free, and easy. Instead of thanking your referring friends after everything is done, try this.

How Future Referrals/Recommendations Are Reinforced, Rewarded, and Assured

Let's take a logical look at how we can foster the free flow of future referrals.

We can begin by remembering we're in the people business, which means we are in the relationship business. As humans, we deepen our relationships by fulfilling our natural desires for feelings of significance, and a sense of certainty.

When we receive the gift of referral, it's important to acknowledge and appreciate the generosity of the gift-giver.

Also, we need to keep in mind that when people make a referral/recommendation, they are putting their reputation and social capital on the line. It's important to thank them for placing their confidence in us, and assure them we will do a great job and make them look like a hero for recommending us.

To Foster Repeat Referrals, Do These Two Simple Things:

1. Gush *sincere* appreciation. Reinforce their wise decision to refer you by making a promise. Promise that you will make them look good, smart, and cool for referring and recommending you.
   Keep your promise (duh).

2. Tell them you'll keep them in the loop, and do it. Share appropriate progress and successes throughout the transaction (of course, don't reveal any confidential information or compromise your fiduciary responsibilities). Doing this will please the referrer, plus, because you are having In-Person,

On-Purpose conversations with the very people who are sending you referrals, doing this will also position you to receive additional r ecommendations.

Showing your appreciation and keeping the friends who refer you business in the know is wise on many levels, don't you think? Isn't this what you'd appreciate? Amen again.

Digital Referrals, Recommendations, and Endorsements

It's a new social media era. Remember, when someone Facebook "likes," "shares," or "comments"; re-Tweets, tags, and/or otherwise shares your digital stuff, thank them and when possible, return the favor.

What Next?

From now on, as you receive referrals, show your appreciation, deliver remarkable service, and keep your referring friends informed. They'll love you for it, and share more referrals. Right now, if you're working with clients who were referred to you, and you haven't showered your referring friend with appreciation, reconnect, and come-correct.

Chapter Twenty

How to Simplify Success: The Fix-It or Fire-It Method

"Whatever is happening to YOU now, YOU either created it, YOU allow it or YOU promote it."

~ Unknown

Reread the above quote. It's the naked truth and reality for 97% of what happens to us in our real estate careers. Success, challenges, and setbacks alike, we're personally responsible.

Setting Things Right Is Simple

When we're unhappy with the results we're producing, we can take personal responsibility and reevaluate what, where, and how we do things, and who we're doing them with. Then we can employ The Fix-It or Fire-It Method.

The Fix-It or Fire-It Method
Your Current Listing Inventory Is Not Selling?
Fix-It or Fire-It

To position your listings to sell, there are only three things you can tweak:

1) How attractively the property shows.

2) The competitive pricing position.

3) The marketing (advertising, broadcast, and promotion).

Evaluate these three factors, then **fix** or **fire** like so...

1. **Fix** how the property shows compared to its competition. Recommend appropriate interior and exterior refreshing, remerchandising, and restaging. If the sellers won't help themselves, **fire** them.

2. **Fix** the competitive pricing position of your listing. Present a detailed, in-the-present, pricing market analysis. If the sellers are unable to take logical action and won't help

themselves, **fire** them and go get some new salable listings.

3. **Fix** the competiveness, persuasiveness, and effectiveness of your property promotion, marketing, and advertising. Review copywriting, broadcast, photo, and presentation quality. If *you* are unwilling, or unable to compete and deliver as promised, do yourself and your sellers a favor; release them and **fire** yourself.

Current Buyer Prospects Not Buying? Fix-It or Fire-It

Selling is very simple. When a qualified and motivated buyer finds a property that fits their needs, they buy it. Evaluate these three things, then **fix** or **fire**.

1. Re-qualify your prospects for urgency, motivation, and ability. If your buyer prospects can't or don't need to buy, **fire** them firmly and gently. Don't cut your ties or burn your bridges; stay in touch and nurture the relationship. When and if their circumstances improve, you'll be positioned to help them. Use the **The Three-People Principle** as your guide.

2. Re-examine what you think your prospects are looking for. Re-question and re-confirm your

understanding of their desired amenities, benefits, location, and other important decision-making factors. If you're unwilling to take the time to understand their needs and desires, **fire** yourself and refer them to a colleague.

3. If you believe your prospects are motivated and financially qualified and you feel you understand what they want–and you've shown it to them—and they still aren't buying, uncover the unspoken barrier: resistance, fear, or obstacle. If you can't figure it out and **fix-it**, **fire** yourself, and refer them to a trusted colleague.

Prospecting Activities Attract Phony-Balonies or the Sound of Crickets? Fix-It or Fire-It

1. Examine all your print and direct mail advertising. How much money are you spending? Is it paying for itself, plus a profit? If it's not, **fire-it** and redirect your money.

2. Where are you advertising? How often? Who's your target? What's your message and is it focused and attractive? How many closed transactions has it generated in the last six months?

If it's not profitable, **fix** something about it (the message, the medium, the frequency, the quality), then reevaluate in thirty days. If it's still not attracting prospects, **fire-it.** *Seriously, if it's not profitable, STOP.*

Is Your Leader Really a Loser? Fix-It or Fire-It

Assuming you are committed, dedicated, and motivated, does your leader provide you with the intellectual, emotional, technological support, and leadership required to thrive? If not, attempt to **fix** their shortcomings and talk to them about meeting your needs. If they are unwilling to adapt, **fire** them and partner with a better leader.

If you feel you're working with a bona-fide leader but your success is sketchy, examine your commitment, motivation, strategy, and execution. Then **fix** your future by making the required changes in your behavior, strategy, action, and activity. If you're unwilling to adapt, do your leader, yourself, and your occasional clients a favor: **fire** yourself.

Do Vendors Make You Look Magnificent and Send Referrals? Fix-It or Fire It

Recommending competent lenders, title companies, painters, plumbers, baby sitters, roofers, and service providers is what our clients expect us to do. If the vendors we recommend aren't reliable, courteous, professional, and a source of return referral recommendations, talk to them about your service requirements and your expectation of reciprocal referral recommendations.

If they are unwilling or unable to perform, bang-bang. Next.

Are You Hugging-it-out with Friends or Slugging-it-out with Frenemies? Fix-It or Fire-It

To have friends, you must be a friend. If you are and they aren't, talk to them about how you two can **fix** your relationship. If they are unwilling to be a friend, **fire** them.

If your friends are Debbie Downers, gossipy backstabbers, or two-faced, **fire** them.

If you're a David Downer, gossipy backstabber, or two-faced, **fix** yourself.

Hang and hug-it-out with positive, supportive, bright people. If you're not, begin nurturing new positive and supportive relationships.

Our Shiny Future

As Oprah Winfrey is credited with saying, "We can't become what we need to be by remaining what we are." I've shared six areas where immediate action will yield immediate results. Your listings will sell faster, marketing dollars will work harder, you'll leverage your time with qualified buyers and sellers, you'll enjoy the benefits of competent leadership, and the warmth of true-blue friends will turn your life richer.

I guess the obvious question is, "When do we start?"

Chapter Twenty-One

How to Employ and Enjoy
the Natural Law
of Shared Favors

"Nothing will work, unless you do."

~ Maya Angelou, Poet

Congratulations! People view you as an expert. Hallelujah! You know *correct* is happening. You know, because people are picking up their phones, dialing your number, and asking you for expert answers and solutions to their burning questions and unsolved problems.

Questions Like:

What's the deal with mortgage rates? Should I refinance?

We're sweatin' like swine over here. I need digits for an A/C dude, not some ex-convict; I need someone who knows what they're doin'. Someone who will drop whatever they're workin' on and haul ass over here to fix this broken piece of crap.

I'm getting hosed. These bloodsuckers can't get away with this. I want to protest my property tax and slap-the-stupid out of city hall. How do I do that?

A "For Sale" sign just went up down the street. Can you tell me what they're asking?

And other run-of-the-mill and quirky kinds of questions. Questions that only a plugged-in, kick-ass real estate agent would know the answer to. Which is why they call you.

Hallelujahs are in order. All your sweaty **Top of Mind Awareness** work is paying off. You're not chasing, stalking, or selling anybody. People are calling you direct. Beautiful.

What you do with this phone call is a turning point for you. Will your response be mundane or mighty? Here's what I mean.

The Mundane Exchange

You're sitting at your computer, busy fretting about your red river of advertising expenses. You're hoping your ads pay off, someday, somehow. You murmur a silent prayer, *Please, dear Lord, compel my expensive, limp ads to make my phone ring.*

Gulp. Your phone rings. Wow. You're kinda creeped out, but excited. A past client is calling to ask you those random kind of questions we talked about earlier. You listen lazy, thinking to yourself, *Damn, this isn't the ad call I prayed for, these people won't move for years. This is a freaking interruption.*

You answer their question in a rush. They thank you. You thank them for calling.

Click.

You return to your fretting and the business of bleeding out, as you continue to chase complete strangers. Sigh.

What just happened? Nothing much. And that's the point. The possibility for your success didn't budge. If that's how you answer, you might as well not be in the business. You're blowing off extraordinary opportunities.

So, let's imagine something mighty instead.

A More Mighty Exchange

Your phone rings. It's Jean, a past client. Calling to ask a question. You smile, straighten, and focus.

Jean asks a question. You listen loudly and ask follow-up-with-clarity questions. Before answering, you reinforce Jean's wise decision to call YOU. Everyone loves to be appreciated, so you give Jean a big verbal hug. You say something like, "Thanks for calling, Jean. I know you could have called any number of other real estate agents – I appreciate you calling on me." Jean feels significant, and appreciated. Cool!

You answer Jean's question. You chit-chat. You're attentive and waiting for "*it*." You know "*it*'s" coming.

Predictably, "*It*" happens. Jean concludes with "*Thank you*." At this precise moment you conjure up the win-win-win called The Natural Law of Shared Favors. This natural law states that when one good person does another good person a favor, the good person receiving the favor wants to return the favor. Isn't this true with you?

If I were (and I usually do) keeping The Natural Law of Shared Favors in mind, here's an example of what my conversation with Jean would sound like after we've chit-chatted, I've answered her question(s) and she concludes our conversation with ("*it*"): *Thank you.*

Jean: Thank you, Ken, I appreciate it.

Me: You're welcome, call me any time; I appreciate you thinking of me. You know, Jean, before I let you go, I was wondering if you might do me favor?

Jean: Sure.

Me: Well, let me ask you a question. If one of your neighbors or a friend from work asked you for a real estate agent recommendation, would you be comfortable sharing my name? That would be so appreciated.

Jean: Of course, I'd be happy to.

Me: Thanks so much; that means a lot to me. I promise, when you refer me to someone, I'll treat them like family and take great care of them. Who's the next person in your neighborhood who's gonna be making a move?

It's that simple. Your words may be different, our results the same. We were asked a favor, we delivered a favor, and we provided an opportunity for a return favor.

Can you see how during the course of a year, by moving from the mundane to the mighty, you could uncover hidden opportunities? This doesn't require any extra work, or money. All you have to do is rearrange words when you help people and answer questions.

Remember to amplify the remarkable you. Mail a handwritten note with two of your business cards. Do it immediately. Please.

Wanna weave even more ridiculous and mighty magic? Of course you do. Why not, right? We're on a roll, man!

To Supersize Your Win-Win-Win and Mighty Magic, Do This

You know the service provider person you just referred – the roofer, the painter, the decorator, the accountant – they appreciate referrals as much as you do. It's the lifeblood of their business too. Here's what supersizing success looks and reads like.

After I hang up from talking with Jean, I call them (the service provider I recommended to Jean). I share that I've just got off the phone from referring them to Jean Wycroft and they should expect a call from her. I impress upon them how important Jean is to me and that I trust they will do a magnificent job for her. I instruct them not to contact Jean directly, but to expect her call. I tell them that I want to know how the conversation went and what happened, and to call me after they hear from her. I wish them luck in winning the business. Then I wait for "*it*." When I hear them say, "Thank you," I ask for a return favor.

Them: Thanks for the referral, Ken.

Me: You're welcome – I know you'll do a great job. It's my pleasure. Hey, can I ask you a quick question? It's sort of semi-personal.

Them: Ummm, sure. What is it?

Me: Well, John, in your day-to-day business you're in contact with a lot of people. I know people trust your work and your opinion. I was wondering, if someone asked you for the name of a trustworthy real estate agent, whose name would you share?

I've asked a direct, on purpose, I'm not pussy-footing around question. I quietly wait for their answer. It might be natural to feel a little pushy asking this question; it sort of puts this person on the spot. Yeah, it sort of does, but in this case, I'm referring this person profitable business opportunities, so I'm being bold about asking for return referrals. Bashful real estate agents starve, bold real estate agents thrive.

Their answer can go two ways.

Way One

Them: Well Ken, you know my wife's brother's uncle's second cousin is our family real estate agent.   My wife would kill me if I didn't recommend her. I hope you understand?

Me: No worries at all. I know we all appreciate loyalty, so I respect that. If you or anyone else ever needs a second opinion, or I can help with anything, I'd be happy to do it. Okay then, let me know when you hear from Jean, and how it went.

In this case, I don't resist or insist. I listen and courteously position myself for future referrals should anything go wrong or their distant relative exits the business.

Way Two

Them: Well, Ken, I'd recommend you of course.

Me: Thanks so much; that means a lot to me. I promise, when you refer me to someone, I'll treat them like family and take great care of them. Who's the next person you know who is making a move?

As always, when I'm sharing my directionally correct dialogues, your words may be different but our winning results will be the same. In this case, like many of the others, we aren't chasing strangers, we aren't annoying friends, we aren't buying ads or stalking people, we're taking an everyday situation and instead of mundaneing our way through the motions, we're attentive, engaging, and speaking our way to success.

Oh, and don't forget to mail Jean and John a handwritten note, inserting two business cards.

Chapter Twenty-Two

How to Dipping Bird Your Way to Perpetual Referrals.

"They say that time changes things, but you actually have to change them yourself."

~ Andy Warhol

The Dipping Bird

You've seen a Dipping Bird, haven't you? Some wonder how it works. It appears to be a perpetual motion machine.

To set the Dipping Bird in motion, you place the bird next to a glass of water. Gently push the bird's head forward so that it barely touches the water, then let go. Its head will then rise and dip perpetually. Or so it seems.

How does this happen? There are no batteries or power sources, yet the bird continues to dip and rise, dip and rise. For hours. It's remarkable and people think it's a magic trick. But it's not.

The Dipping Bird is a smart combination of heat vaporization, torque, center of mass physics, capillary action, and combined gases chemistry. What appears to be perpetual motion is, in reality, a simple combination of science (the invisible: natural laws, and physics), and clever art (the visible: packaging and presentation).

If you want to, you can use a similar proven formula to generate perpetual referral recommendations. But instead of physics, your ingredients are an understanding of human behavior, timing, conversation, and follow-up. Just like the little Dipping Bird drinks and rises, drinks and rises, if you put what you learn in this chapter into action, every time you take a new listing, or begin to work with buyer clients, you'll generate one or two new referrals before the transaction closes. Imagine the positive impact on your success if every time you worked with a qualified buyer or seller, you earned a new qualified buyer or seller referral.

First let's take a look at how most agents commonly behave; then we'll dive into how to Dipping Bird your way to perpetual referrals.

Here's What Most Agents Are Doing Wrong Now

They take a new listing or begin working with a homebuyer. They work super hard, keep their promises, and the listing sells or the buyer buys.

During the escrow period, as per usual, there are a few unexpected hiccups, but diligence prevails and everything goes well. The closing takes place on schedule. Everyone's happy. Yeah!

Generally, if it happens at all, it happens after closing. The average and ordinary agent commonly asks for a referral recommendation after the closing.

The Problem with This Strategy Is . . .

During the transaction, buyers and sellers are all a-twitter about real estate. They're swapping real estate experiences, asking and answering questions, and sharing their stories with everyone they talk to. During the transaction, they're hyper-aware of friends who are also thinking of making a move.

By waiting to timidly ask for referral recommendation until *after* the transaction closes, the agent is missing out on hearing about any juicy opportunities their clients might share with them *during* the transaction. If only they were asked.

Remember, these clients are talking to everyone about their experience. If you're delivering excellent service and results, they would be happy to refer you, if only you would ask. The key to creating Dipping Bird referral recommendations is to ask for referral recommendations *during* the transaction, *not after*.

The Dipping Bird Referral Strategy Goes Like This

1. Attract a paying customer – I know, duh.

---

2. Make your compelling, persuasive presentation of services (listing or buyer's representation presentation/consultation.)

3. After you're chosen and the listing/buyer agreements are signed, shake hands and exchange smiles.   Then, as you're leaving, or at the end of your next conversation, pause, thank them again and in your own words share that you appreciate their trust and confidence, and you'll keep all your promises or they can fire you on the spot. And that to make sure you're staying on track and they're pleased, from time to time you're going to ask them how you're doing.

Example: *Thanks again for your confidence, I appreciate it. Listen, if at any time you feel I'm not living up to my promises, you can fire me, no questions asked, no hard feelings, and no fees. To make sure you're happy with everything I'm doing and that I'm on track. I'm going to check in with you from time to time and ask you, straight up, how I'm doing and if you're happy.*

In addition to making this the best home selling experience you've ever had, I want to create a experience where, if a friend, neighbor, or coworker asked you how it's going, I want my work performance to be at a level where you would say, "Man oh man, Ken Brand is awesome, he's keeping all his promises and more." So, I'll *be checking with you, okay?*

4. The hard part: Deliver. Crazy. Audacious. On time. As promised. In steps 1 – 4 you've positioned yourself to conversationally ask for referrals and recommendations during the transaction. This will be simple and natural, because you've set the stage for it.

   Deliver strong, wait for their *"Thank you,"* and take these next steps.

5. When your clients experience a positive event and say *"Thank you,"* for example, after progress reports, showing appointments, contract presentation, contract negotiations, or option period expirations, respond naturally and say something like, "Thanks for the compliment, you're welcome!"

6. Immediately follow this up with something like, "It sounds like you're pleased and things are going well?" and remind them of your earlier conversation (Step 3), then ask for a referral recommendation.

   It might sound something like this:

   Them: Thanks for the <u>insert positive event,</u> Ken.

Me: Thanks for the compliment; you're welcome. I don't know if you remember this or not, but when we first got started, we were sitting at the kitchen table and I said that my goal was to create the best experience you've ever had? I know we're not done yet but it sounds like, so far, things are on track and you're happy?

Them: Yes.

Me: Great. Can I ask you this? If a friend or a neighbor needed some real estate help and asked you for a recommendation, do you think you'd be comfortable sharing my name?

Them: Sure, Ken, you're doing a fine job.

Me: Yeah, thanks! Rest assured, when you refer me to someone, I promise I'll take great care of them, treat them like family, and make you look good for recommending me. So, let me ask you this. Of your friends at work/in the neighborhood/at the gym/etc. [pick one small group], who's the next person to make a move?

7. If they share a referral, congratulations. If they don't, no worries. Thank them and rock on. Lather, rinse, and repeat Steps 5, 6, and 7 at every significant positive milestone that includes and concludes with their enthusiastic *"Thank you for a job well done.* I imagine you might ask five or seven times during the transaction.

Does It Work?

Yes, it does! If you have clients, you do a fantastic job, and they say "*Thank you,*" then you have earned the privilege of asking for referral recommendations during the transaction. Do it!

If you're asking for referrals infrequently, awkwardly at closing – or worse, sometime after closing, you're self-strangling your prosperity. Stop doing that and do this instead.

Follow Steps 1 – 3 and you will have natural and comfortable opportunities to ask for referral recommendations, conversationally and respectfully.

Follow Steps 4 – 7 and your delighted clients will be happy to refer their friends, family members, and coworkers.

Follow Steps 1 – 7 and you'll Dipping Bird your way to perpetual referrals.

Let me share a word about scripts and preparation. If you're reluctant, skeptical, or become ill at the thought of memorizing and reciting scripts, I hear you. I'm not advocating the use of my words; I'm sharing directionally-correct dialogues as examples.

While I don't encourage or even use scripts *per se*, I do encourage you to study the directionally correct dialogue examples in this book, then create and rehearse your own directionally-correct dialogues (as I do). I'm a believer in perfect practice and preparation using rehearsed, directionally-correct dialogues when appropriate. The more familiar you are with what you're going to say, the more persuasive, crisp, confident, and beneficial your conversation will be.

Making this slight shift in strategy is the easy part. If you do this, you will position yourself to speak perpetual referrals into existence. The hard part is keeping your promises and delivering referral-worthy results. I know you can do both, especially since you've already read so much of this book already and have put so much of the advice you've received into place.

Chapter Twenty-Three

How to Keep That-Other-Woman from Seducing Your People

"In marketing you must choose between boredom, shouting and seduction. Which do you want?"

~ Roy H. Williams, Author

It's Not Personal. It's Business

Listen. That-Other-Woman. All the people you know, she knows. Everyone knows more than one good real estate agent, right?

She knows you're a respected, savvy, and well-connected pro, but that's not going to stop her. She sees herself as equally attractive and more than capable. To succeed, she knows she has to out-delight, surprise, and engage you. She has plans to seduce your people, steal your opportunity, and your future.

Next week, while waiting for your ho-hum direct mail postcard to land on their kitchen table, along with all the other irritating junk mail, she'll be inviting everyone you know to two hours of movie star bedazzle and Technicolor® surround sound.

She's one in 500, and she's inviting your friends, clients, suspects, and prospects to a Hollywood Blockbuster.

Don't tell her, but I was able to put my hands on her plan. Here's what she's doing – check it out.

Movie Day Action Plan

Monday Morning

1. Log on to the local multi-screen mega theatre website.

2. Check the movie schedule, pick a movie and a showtime. (Wednesday or Thursday, noonish matinee if possible.)

3. Write a fun e-mail invitation. Include a picture of the movie poster. Send to everyone. Remember to use Bcc box. (Top Secret copy of her e-mail at the end of this chapter. You can do way better, I'm sure.)

Tuesday Afternoon/Evening

1. Call all. Say hello. Confirm receipt. Personally invite. Chitchat. Let conversational magic bloom. Share excitement for a "yes," express regrets for a "no" (either way, the "Halo Effect" shines its soft blessing on her relationship).

2. Follow up all my conversations with a short, handwritten note card. Mail with two biz cards.

Wednesday – 11:15am

Meet everyone at the movies. Yay! Wear real estate name badge. Greet everyone with a big smile and a warm "welcome" hug. Hand out movie tickets. Can't wait to hear, "*Thank you so much, how thoughtful. I needed a break. You're the greatest friend and REALTOR® of all time.*"

Bring digital camera (smart phone camera). Take pictures. Go inside and enjoy the movie.

Say goodbye. Give more hugs, say goodbye, and wish everyone well. Don't forget to thank everyone for coming.

Wednesday Evening.

Post and share "We're having fun!" pictures to Facebook and Flickr accounts and Blog.

Write fun post-movie follow-up e-mail. Include pictures of grinning attendees and a link to your Facebook photo album. Tweet about it too. Send an e-mail to all invited, thank those who came, tell those who couldn't make it we missed them, and wish everyone well.

Those Were Her Typed Notes, and Here Are Her Mental Notes

I'll never mention real estate unless asked, but my e-mail invitations are wrapped in my real estate branded e-mail stationery. This movie event won't cost much, postage is free, there are zero printing costs. Even if fifty people show up—and there'll probably be fewer than that; twenty-five would be great—the whole thing will cost less than $300.

This movie event is way funner than wasting $300 on some dumb print ad in a real estate magazine, trying to chase strangers and attract KuKu birds.

Whether people can attend or not, everyone appreciates a generous gesture, and who doesn't love-love an invitation to have fun? The Halo Effect is going to shine a perfect light. Yeah!

While other agents are doing next to nothing, cutting back, or sending routinely ho-hum post cards, you'll be giving the gift of entertainment and enjoyment. People will talk about your invitation and the movie. Yay for you and your friends.

This movie event gives us the chance to touch people five times in one week: by e-mail invitation, phone call follow-up, handwritten note card follow-up, in person at the movies, and a post movie follow-up e-mail. Plus, we'll have some fun pictures to share on Facebook, and Flickr.

So, She's Taking Your Good People on a Date. What Will You Do About It?

Like I said, only one in 500 people will do this. The question is, will that one in 500 be doing it with your soon-to-be-seduced friends, clients, prospects, and suspects? Or are you that unique one in 500 who won't let that happen?

For you one in 500s, let me know how it goes. Drop me an e-mail at Ken@KenBrand.com For the other 499, I'm sorry.

P.S. Don't overthink or overplan this. You could pull this off next week.

P.S. Here's that e-mail invitation I was telling you about.

Let's Go See Brad Pitt in Benjamin Buttons - My Treat
1 message

Ken Brand <brandk@garygreene.com>   Mon, Dec 15, 2008 at 2:29 PM
To: Ken Brand <kens411@gmail.com>

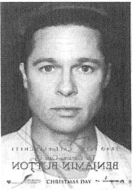

Happy New Year – I'm taking my friends to go see **Brad Pitt in Benjamin Button** and you're invited. The holiday season has been exhausting, let's enjoy a two hour entertainment break with Brad.

It'll be a fun time, it's my treat, **I'm buying your movie ticket.**

Here's the deal: We'll attend the matinee, **Wednesday Morning, January 7th, 2009. Our movie starts at 11:30am,** so I'll be standing just inside the front door at 11:00am, with your ticket. The movie is showing at: **Cinemark at Market Street** /9595 Six Pines Dr., The Woodlands, TX 77380. The show should be over by 1:47pm

Hopefully, you can join us. I'd like to get a friend count for tickets, if you would, **please hit the reply button and give me thumbs "UP" or "Down".**

I look forward to seeing you, call if you have any questions. My cell is: 832-797-1779

Cheers and Happy New Year.

Ken:-)

Ken Brand
O 281 367 3531
C 832 797 1779
Blog Kens411.com
BrandK@GaryGreene.com

GaryGreene.com

Chapter Twenty-Four

Thirty-Two How-tos
for Three Types of Real Estate
Agents

*"It used to be that the big ate the small.
Now the fast eat the slow."*

~ Geoff Yang

I wanted to close my book with one of my most post popular articles at AgentGenius.com. Also I'd like to express my heartfelt thanks to Benn and Lani Rosales. Benn is the founder and Lani is the new media director for the award-winning online real estate magazine, AgentGenius.com. If you're not an AgentGenius.com reader today, I encourage you to bookmark or subscribe to their daily dose of insight, what's new, how-to and what's next in the real estate business. Run, don't walk to www. AgentGenius.com

Thank you again to Benn and Lani, my fellow AG writers, friends, and readers. Here you go. . .

There Are Three Types of Real Estate Agents.

1. Those that have forgotten more bright ideas than they can remember.

2. Those filling their heads with all the new bright ideas they can find.

3. Those that have both forgotten more than they can remember and are always on the lookout for new bright ideas.

There Are Three Types of Challenges for All Real Estate Agents

First, the status quo will not maintain your business.

The second challenge is a choice challenge; choosing solid gold ideas and strategies over fool's gold.

The third challenge? Moving our chosen ideas out of the imaginary feel-good world of good intentions and into the real world arena of action, implementation, and monetization.

Whichever Type You Are...

I thought these ideas were solid gold and were realistically simple to implement. I plucked these from a <u>fifty-nine page list</u> of Twitter-sized ideas submitted by attendees at <u>Prudential Real Estate's Top Producer Summit</u> conference. Here they are.
. .

1. Use video chat to meet your relocation clients face-to-face often before they relocate! Be the source of the source!

2. Find an article, fact, or something at least once a week to post on your blog or Facebook.

3. Start networking in your office! Know your team.

4. Offer to sponsor the local high school play! Print their programs in exchange for your contact info on the back!

5. Volunteer to read one day a month at a senior home/school.

6. Buy an external hard drive and back up your computer weekly.

7. Be the water stop sponsor for a local running group.

8. Send a "Welcome to your new home" card to the new buyer who purchased your listing, and add them to your mailing list. Even if they weren't your buyer.

9. Always wear a name badge.

10. Communicate with your clients based on how they communicate with you.

11. Every day that you don't prospect, ask yourself "Why?" and refuse to use that excuse again.

12. Send lots of personal notes.

13. Hire a professional photographer to take your listing photos.

14. Add free Wi-Fi for all buyer agents when visiting any of your listings.

15. Pick one new tool or technology to learn each week and become an expert.

16. Start every day with a clear and measurable goal. Know what a successful day looks like before your feet hit the floor.

17. Remember anyone can be a client, so be kind when you meet people.

18. A thank you goes so much farther when it is handwritten.

19. When your buyer has completely moved into their new home, offer to throw a housewarming party for them. Let them invite twenty of their top friends. You, the agent, can buy the food and, of course, a nice bottle of wine. Homeowners buy drinks. Now you are there at their party.

20. It's a price war. Keep getting price reductions.

21. Instead of a sign rider saying "Call me," it should say "Text me for info on this house!!

22. Create e-mail signatures for the things you send out often.

23. SlideShare.com.

24. Ask your clients how they would like you to communicate with them. Some prefer e-mail, some phone, others only text.

25. Surround yourself with people that support your goals and who are fearless.

26. We cannot control the market. We can control our attitude and focus. Become the agent that buyers and sellers seek to make things happen!

27. When I get a buyer, I send a mock offer to them right away. Then when I see them or talk to them again, I review it with them. It allows us the chance to answer all questions or concerns before we write the final offer.

28. Stop making excuses and devote five hours a week to prospecting.

29. A busy day doesn't mean a good day if you haven't reached out to five to ten clients in your database of recent contacts.

30. In order not to be overwhelmed on my cell phone with inquiries, and to separate new folks from signed clients, I use a unique telephone number from Google Voice. Messages are transcribed and sent to e-mail, or a number can be forwarded to your assistant.

31. Luck is predictable. If you want more luck, take more chances, show up more often, try more things.

32. Send closing sheets copy (HUD) to clients in January from previous year's closings.

Remember, Knowing What Others Don't and Doing What Others Won't Are the True Two Secrets to Success

I encourage you to implement at least one thing from this list of thirty-two and one idea from a chapter in this book per week. They say it takes twenty-one repetitions to create a new habit; keep that in mind in your quest for sweet success. If you have some ideas or comments you'd like to share, Twitter-sized or otherwise, please send them in an e-mail Ken@KenBrand.com

Final Thoughts

Thanks for reading my book. We've covered a lot of new ground together. It's a hyper-competitive marketplace these days, and you simply can't sit still for even a day. If you'll take some of what you've learned about behavior, strategy, activities, and actions and put it into *doing what others won't* practice, I know you'll radically shift your business from Blah-Blah to Ah-Ha. With all the great things you're capable of, you can't be stopped if you start now.

I wish you grace, speed, and sweet success

Ken B.

About the Author

At age four, at 3:42 p.m. on <u>Christmas Eve, he set fire to his home playing pirate in his living room</u>. It's fitting that things have come full circle. Ken's eager to help **you** spark **your** success, **fly your flag**, burn down convention, help you explore **uncharted territories,** and discover your **buried troves of treasure**.

A coach, mentor, parent, **amateur athlete**, gadget guy, **real estate psychologist,** and self-taught **social media anthropologist**, Ken's been involved in more than 16,200 transactions since 1978 in **San Diego, Austin, Aspen**, and in Robyn's and his current home, in **The Woodlands**, Texas.

Through both **spectacular failures** and shared **triumphant victories**, Ken's seen, heard, and most importantly – **felt it all**.

Now that their three kids have scattered across the country to live and learn, he's **eager** to **listen** and **advise, coach and counse**l, commit and (in all likelihood) be committed.

When not helping, Ken's typically floor-burning up the racquetball court or **unearthing third gravitating bodies** in films, books, social media, the majesty of life's daily spectacle, or **his own murmured musings** on his own blog BrandCandid.com or as a guest writer at AgentGenius.com

Here's some stuff copied from his Facebook.com/KenBrand profile page:

Activities: Reading. Wizard Academy. Racquet Ball. Movies. Surfing poorly. Visiting the kids. Vegas of course. Naps. Writing. Music. Social Media. Real Estate Coaching. Working Out. Presenting. Thinking and Day Dreaming. Creating.

Favorite Music: I'm all over the place. Of course real Rock 'n Roll. Some new stuff.

Favorite TV Shows: HBO Series – Sopranos, Deadwood (Al Swerigen reminds me of my dad). OZ, The Wire, Entourage, Six Feet Under, Weeds, Rome, Big Love, Deadliest Catch, and The Antiques Roadshow (weird, I know.). What I don't like is watching the news...all that doom, gloom, and woe-is-us stuff makes me go uggg.

Favorite Movies: Braveheart, The Big Lebowski, Forrest Gump, Pulp Fiction, Schindler's List, Memento, Reservoir Dogs, Perfume, Ace Ventura, The Shawshank Redemption, True Romance, Band of Brothers, Little Miss Sunshine, Gladiator, The Hurt Locker, Crazy Heart, The Wizard of Oz.

Favorite Writers: Seth Godin, Tom Peters, Roy H. Williams, John Irving, Phillip Roth, Edgar Rice Burroughs, Isaac Asimov, Robert Ludlum, Tim Robbins, Roy H. Williams, Jeff Sexton, Brian Solis.

Work – Live – Play: Residential real estate solutions, bright ideas, candid consultations, anti-chaos systems, elite performance coaching, creative communication arts solutions, and thirty-two years of fun, shared triumph, boom, bust, blood, sweat and tears experience. Ken is the sales manager for an award-winning team of real estate agent icons at Prudential Gary Greene, Realtors – The Woodlands Area Regional Marketing and Sales Center.

You can connect with Ken here:

BrandCandid.com

Facebook.com/BrandCandid

Twitter.com/KenBrand

linkedin.com/in/kenbrand

16552253R00144

Made in the USA
Charleston, SC
27 December 2012